THE BAD TEMPERED GARDENER

THE BAD TEMPERED GARDENER

Anne Wareham
Photographs by Charles Hawes

F
FRANCES LINCOLN LIMITED
PUBLISHERS

For Charles with love. Without you, nothing.

HALF TITLE PAGE A cut-out dove (or pigeon) at the end of the yew walk, with *Persicaria campanulata* Alba Group in flower.
TITLE PAGE The crescent border and the pool in July, with *Nectaroscordum siculum*, *Alchemilla mollis*, *Campanula lactiflora* and unknown water lilies.

Frances Lincoln Limited
4 Torriano Mews
Torriano Avenue
London NW5 2RZ
www.franceslincoln.com

The Bad Tempered Gardener
Copyright © Frances Lincoln Limited 2011
Text copyright © Anne Wareham 2011
Photographs copyright © Charles Hawes 2011
pp. 6-7 Veddw House garden plan copyright © Elizabeth Buckley
www.elizabethbuckleygardens.co.uk

First Frances Lincoln edition 2011

A catalogue record for this book is available from the British Library.

978 0 7112 3150 4

Printed and bound in China

1 2 3 4 5 6 7 8 9

CONTENTS

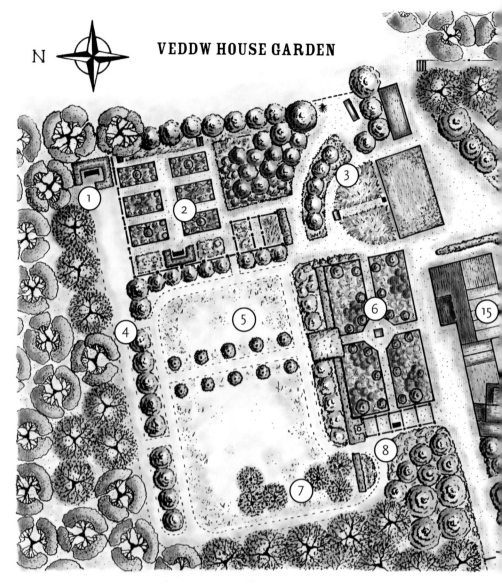

VEDDW HOUSE GARDEN

N

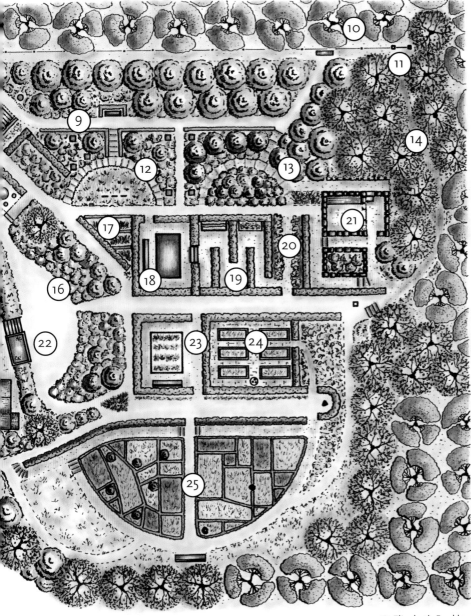

© Elizabeth Buckley

18 Pool Garden	22 Pond
19 Hedge Garden	23 New Garden
20 Hosta Walk	24 Cornfield Garden
21 Ruin	25 Grasses Parterre

INTRODUCTION

I am a square peg in a round hole and just as uncomfortable as that sounds. I have to make my way in a world which is totally alien to me. A world where people are inevitably passionate, always 'green' and always terribly concerned about the little furry things – and even the little slimy things sometimes. It's a busy world, both visually and literally, which invents, admires and perpetuates hard work. But, paradoxically, it appears to be fast asleep. I attempt to waken the garden world up but it deeply resents my shaking it.

I began, of course, like everyone else. My first gardening attempts were on a bit of flat roof on the block of flats where I was living and I climbed in and out of a window to set up and then care for a miniature vegetable plot of pots. A few years later, thoroughly addicted to growing things, I was tackling two acres with a spade and a compulsion. I read everything I could lay hands on and I visited every garden I could. And, as I and the garden matured, my perspective changed.

I began to get tired of hearing every garden described as 'lovely'. I visited many of them and often found them to be banal and uninspired. I began to wish for writers who would tell the truth about the gardens and gardening and found only 'garden stories' and discussions of gardening techniques which were totally foreign to me and as much use to me as learning how to lay an egg. I got bored of reading endless descriptions of plants and very little useful guidance as to how to use them together. I became impatient, because I could find intelligent and challenging ideas in all sections of newspapers and magazines except the garden sections. Even the *Spectator*, spiky, cconfrontational and outspoken, let me down. The misnamed 'gardens' section' is in fact almost always about gardening and is indistinguishable from the gardening columns you will find in the politest newspaper or magazine. This is not the columnists' responsibility – they keep meticulously to their brief. The problem is the fond idea that gardening is inevitably nice but dull. It seems that no editor ever imagines it could be otherwise.

I've succeeded in becoming the elephant in the garden. People know I'm there, galumphing about and making trouble, but on the whole the garden world prefers to pretend all is well and the wild animals are still safely locked up. I've galumphed a bit in print, and on television, and I think that some people are beginning to think there is something to be said for a more critical look at gardens, but it's a

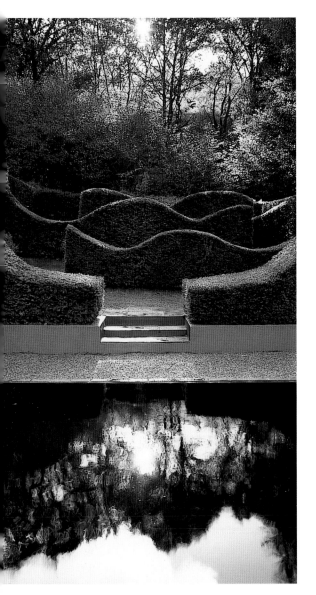

long struggle and it may well come to nothing.

So my picture is this: that there will, at some remote point in the future be someone else, also making a garden – someone else with a demanding vision and a need to express that vision in competition with and collusion with the seasons, the weather, the light and the elusive flowering and destruction wrought by time. Someone without banal reverence for 'nature' and 'greenness' but who recognizes that working with nature is a serious game, where we can party but the party will continue without all of us once our game is ended.

This rather lonely person will find this book, in some form, in the equivalent of the second-hand bookshop, and they will no longer feel alone. They may even feel heartened to take up the struggle again. And perhaps the world may then be ready and gardens will blossom again as a serious and even outrageous art form.

The reflecting pool, reflecting the hedge garden and coppice, just as it should.

THE BEGINNINGS

Making a garden for me has been about making a place for myself in alien worlds. I am an outsider in the garden media world, and when we first came to the Veddw we were also outsiders in our immediate geographical world. I am by nature an outsider who continually struggles for acceptance, so I tend to begin my forays into alien worlds by trying to find myself a place. So it was in the Veddw.

This part of the Welsh border is strange not so much because it is Welsh but because it was, for me, an unfamiliar kind of countryside and very hard to make sense of. The conventional picture of the 'country' in the UK is of sweet and cosy villages, surrounded by farmland. Here, I found myself surrounded by a multitude of tiny settlements, rather odd villages and very ugly houses, which were mostly people's mixed responses to trying to make old squatter and agricultural cottages into what might be considered acceptable housing in the late twentieth century.

We had also come to this part of the world in a very abrupt and arbitrary way. I was looking for land enough to make a real garden, as opposed to the relatively tiny garden I had in London. I knew, having gardened for a few years, that this was a serious part of my life and that a hundred yards of London garden was not going to satisfy me for ever: I needed more scope.

The first place we looked was the Peak District, because we had friends there and good possibilities for work for my then partner, now husband, Charles. We were at the point of exchanging contracts on our London house when we discovered that we would be refused planning permission to make the kind of garden we were envisaging in the Peak District National Park. We suddenly had to decide whether to give up the whole enterprise. So looking on the Welsh border was very much a last-ditch attempt to do something which seemed quite crazy anyway, given that Charles didn't want to move and we had very little money.

Charles drew a circle on a road map in a part of the world he knew vaguely from his student days in Bristol and told me to try there. It was just in Wales, and we had an idea that property was cheaper in Wales. The message from Charles was definitely 'last chance'.

We came down that weekend, saw the Veddw and decided we could settle for the place. We did not fall in love with the rather shabby, unattractive house or really recognize at that point how perfect the land was for our purpose. It would do.

So we bought in haste out of necessity. We knew no one. This is not a Welsh part of Wales, the language is English, but we still felt very uncomfortable in this strange landscape. It all felt very arbitrary, as if we'd been dropped randomly from a balloon. Our first year here was the worst of our lives together and settling in took time and effort. Our comfort and refuge had always been our local pub but the one in Devauden at the time felt like something out of Thomas Hardy. A single room, like someone's old cottage sitting room, where cider was served to clannish locals who all stared when you walked in and muttered a rather unfriendly greeting. Any conversation was public, audible to the whole room. We were like fish in a septic tank.

So I had to make a garden out of two acres of grassland, and I had to find a way to feel at home. Let's start with the garden.

Charles insisted we must grow vegetables. This is somewhat ironic, since we eventually gave that up. So I started by beginning to dig in a corner of the lower field. At that point I had no plan and was slightly intimidated by the idea of digging the whole two acres (we bought the woods, doubling the size, a couple of years later). I got stuck in, nevertheless.

But when I went indoors or visited shops I researched like mad, convinced there had to be an alternative to digging the whole plot. And I discovered mulching, by way of a wonderful American (Ruth Stout) who buried her whole garden in hay, two feet deep, and swore it solved every garden problem, including many I did not have and had difficulty imagining: racoons, gophers . . . I also found it hard to imagine an attractive garden buried two feet deep in hay, but I got the drift and the effort of digging was replaced by the effort of discovering suitable mulches and getting them on site in very large quantities. So, despite the bizarre fact that we recently appeared in a book called *Luxury Gardens*, our beginnings were not just modest but quite revolting, comprising large areas of ground covered with bits of old carpets, newspaper weighed down with planks, old manure and sawdust. But we were away.

Not without conflict. Charles is inclined by nature to make haste slowly, 'finishing what you have begun' before moving on to the next bit. My messy, ambitious and land-conquering efforts regularly resulted in exasperated explosions about the mess. My sense of shame and humiliation was tempered by my frustration at having so little help – while always telling myself, quite accurately, that this was my self-imposed project and I had no right to expect anyone else to join in. It's just that it frequently seemed hopeless. At no time did I ever contemplate stopping. I have no idea why. I didn't, after all, have a clear vision for a long time, nor was I plant addicted. I don't trust any explanation that I might produce for your benefit. I only know nothing deflected me and a good many things militated against the project. And now I have finally succeeded in creating a rod for our backs and a constant financial drain. Work that one out.

The thing spread into all areas of our lives. We visited gardens for a day out or on holiday and Charles was as alongside as anyone sane could be. A professional photographer came one day and told Charles, who had a kind of latent interest in photography, that his camera would be quite adequate for garden photographs. Next thing Charles was up to his neck taking and struggling to sell garden pictures.

I saw a two-hour 'course' on writing for magazines, attended and bought a copy of the *Writers' and Artists' Yearbook* – which encouraged me to approach the *Financial Times*, as, if I remember rightly, it said that not many people did approach them. They took some pieces by me and I got into the whole agony and occasional pleasure of getting into print (the development of another inexplicable and compulsive behaviour). Eventually I learned never to read what was printed and a lot of pain was saved. But writing and photography are another story, yet to come . . .

INFLUENCES

GARDENS

If anyone ever tries to understand what influenced the design and planting at the Veddw I wonder how clear they will be able to be? Clearer than I am. I am inevitably of my own time and therefore, presumably, confluent with the ideas and preoccupations of my time – the formative time being the late twentieth century, because by now (2007) the garden is almost finished, whatever finished means (in this case all the spaces filled with what we currently want to have in them, like finishing a jigsaw puzzle).

I was living in London when I first became interested in gardens, and I visited the gardens accessible from there. Sissinghurst, of course. I have no idea what I learnt. I remember looking at a rather gone-over rose with unsatisfactory underplanting and reflecting that if they had trouble keeping perfection going here then the rest of us could maybe fret less. Though I never have (fretted less). I remember mostly feeling confused and puzzled, which is the way new learning usually takes me. And, I have concluded, it is the way new learning should be, so I find it easier to accept the bewilderment and confusion than I did when I was young. If I'm actually learning something, it is presumably reworking my preconceived ideas, changing my world and generally challenging me. How could this be anything but bewildering and difficult? Naturally, it makes me feel totally inadequate: a feeling which returns with depressing regularity and which alternates unfortunately with grandiosity. (I have been told that an utter inability to gauge one's skills and abilities and a tendency to veer between believing oneself to be queen of the world and a worm is a function of low self-esteem. This idea gave me a tiny momentary grasp of reality and of my likely mediocrity until the whole world was discovered to be suffering from low self-esteem and I gave it up as a bad job. That's all of us, then.)

The Sissinghurst visit must have come at the time when I was looking up 'ground cover' in an attempt to discover what I could use to cover the bare soil under a hardy geranium, only to discover that hardy geraniums were supposed to *be* ground cover. I had a relatively large London garden – maybe a hundred yards long and the house width wide – and it seemed an enormous area to deal with, while clearly limiting my choices in many ways too. Not directly comparable with

'Strong shapes and patterns' – in yew, beech and box: expensive to maintain but a joy all year.

the gardens I was visiting in terms of scale and possibilities. So some bewilderment was no doubt simply to do with the impossibility of rendering these models in small scale, which is what we are encouraged to do. However, I was no doubt learning something.

I learnt, for example, what I didn't want. We visited Beth Chatto's garden in Essex, after I had carefully studied her planting ideas, derived to some degree from flower arrangement and involving triangles. The idea being that an island bed would have a towering plant with lower layers working up to it, as if in a vase. I went and studied the result and decided that this was not the kind of form I was interested in. The vase was the only strong shape I could identify. The paths meandered. The beds were a sort of indeterminate shape. I realized, but did not remember later, that I wanted strong shapes and pattern, straight lines, squares and circles – because they satisfy and please me.

I say I forgot: when we first began the garden at the Veddw I asked a local nurserywoman, the much-loved Charlotte Evans, to come and advise me. Which she did for an afternoon, for £17. And I re-learnt what I *didn't* want. Charlotte, who at that time had a famous nursery and garden at Bully Hole Bottom, a couple of miles away from us, is a plantswoman and a specialist in shrubs. She envisaged groups of shrubs shaping the landscape, creating a garden which is generally known as 'naturalistic'. I immediately remembered my love of straight lines. This is not a frivolous observation: I learnt from Charlotte what I needed, which was that I actually had a strong model to draw on, and the fact that it wasn't hers was not terribly significant. It clarified my thinking and gave me confidence (some) in my own preference.

Presumably I was carrying the images I had acquired from my garden visits. Hidcote is the only other one I remember, though. I remember the mass planting of fuchsia before the swimming pool, and once again being confused. I think because I had never seen or imagined such a planting before, though I suspect they were not yet in flower and that my imagination failed me. I have the distinct impression now that visitors often feel bewildered at the Veddw. I gather this is frequently about the weeds, but I wonder too if it is also that feeling, less easy to articulate, that 'this is not what I expected and I don't quite understand what it is about.'

In attempting all this learning I had and have a major handicap, which is also difficult to express. I seem incapable of taking in or remembering detail. I become shamefully aware of this at the Chelsea Flower Show every year, when my colleagues refer to gardens which I have seen but totally fail to recognize from their detailed descriptions of the planting and even, heaven help me, the structures and form. What on earth am I looking at? And when I'm looking, what on earth do I see? I have only a vague idea. Though it is often a powerful idea – a strong sense of liking or not liking. And at best – with Christopher Bradley-Hole's work, for example – that familiar bewilderment. An inability to understand what is going on and how it is done. I will study the planting, try hard to take in the materials and structures, and I will try, shamefully, to find something intelligent to say. But mostly I am overawed, bewildered – and sure that I could not get to the bottom of this garden without living with it for a week. And being able to wander in it, which is not usually possible.

At this year's Chelsea it was revealed to me that other people do not particularly wish to hear intelligent conclusions, so I am rather wasting my efforts to understand in order to have something intelligent to say (though is it actually easier to find something banal to say?). I was told, gently and tactfully, that people will mostly find such conclusions, however tortuously arrived at, not so much illuminating as uncomfortable and challenging. Me too. But I love challenge and need it as I fumble around in this strange world.

I suppose that the strong lines and shapes I love in my own garden help the chronically bewildered. They give clarity and enable me to see what is going on. And pattern, which is the other thing I find so satisfying and look for over and over, is also clarifying. It is order, it is comprehensible, it is pleasing in an altogether primitive and childlike way.

I do also remember visiting Great Dixter. And what I remember most, apart from being sharply told not to walk on the grass and consequently feeling very stupid and delinquent, was a disconcerting sense of a lack of boundary. I loved that straight path to a delightful porch with amazing pots of plants, loved the strong gardens (straight lines and circles) and the unattainable pavings and buildings around the house. But it all seemed to fade away to nothing; there was nothing at the edges, no sense of containment to the garden as a whole. This troubled me but I imagine would trouble not at all anyone living there. One is inevitably familiar with one's own boundaries and that knowing must be the containment in itself. So I wonder if the Veddw has just the same failing for people who don't live here? I cannot tell. I tell myself that it blends well with the countryside, as it is, I believe, only when you get to the edges that you see where they are. However, the south side is contained and defined by a strong semicircle of trees, so that here, at least, is containment, a sense of ending. Though, of course, it isn't, because the coppice is beyond, with its boundaries defined by inaccessibility and rabbit fencing.

A visit to Hestercombe, after we had moved to the Veddw, gave me permission to do one of my favourite things, but one I had felt very bad about till then. I have always had the habit in nurseries of alighting on a plant that I already have and love, and instantly wanting this one too, or, ideally, every one they have. I can almost always think of a further use for a plant that is good and does well with me – and of course, if you know what a plant does throughout the season it is that much easier to use it with confidence.

I had always, in a horticultural world obsessed with plant accumulating, felt wrong about this. I had the idea that my garden would become repetitive and uninteresting, and indeed it no doubt is exactly that to the majority of visitors who are looking for new and unusual plants – the cliché of the 1990s and the strapline of every nursery. Hestercombe offered me reassurance. I think it may have been lavender that recurred, but no matter what it was, I saw the same plant repeated, used with wholehearted generosity, and I loved it and knew with excitement that I was right: this was what would support the garden's unity and integrity. I had a familiar switch from humility to assurance – and at these times I always wonder why I don't trust myself more. Suddenly I was free to indulge, and freedom is what it felt like.

Curiously, Hestercombe offered me a further reassurance some years later. I had always looked down on the Great Plat and hated some large grasses which were sticking up in the beds there. They looked awful to me, but I told myself, of course, that this was a Jeykll planting and my judgement must be flawed. Then the garden was given an authentic makeover – and the ugly grasses vanished.

Incidentally, the garden world *adores* nurseries. And, of course they are very worthy, run with a ridiculous amount of hard work to very little profit. I sold plants from the garden for a while and got very disenchanted. One year everyone would ask for *Campanula lactiflora* and I'd run out of it. I would grow extra the next year and not a soul would want one. And weeding the garden is bad enough; weeding plants in pots is absolutely a weeding too far.

However, the nursery habit is at the bottom of the abysmal British garden. That and plant sales at NGS garden openings. All those little specials, all needing to be squeezed in somewhere in an already over-stuffed garden. Strange that greed for clothes (hurray!) or 'consumer goods' (what they?) is vilified as 'consumerism', but greed for plants is applauded.

I'd like to speak up for garden centres. I could do without the plastic furniture, DVDs and tacky souvenirs, but they are the only places where you can actually get a generous amount of plants. At a nursery if you want half a dozen you may find two before being told 'you can't have that, it's the stock plant.' Garden centres tend

A rare but wonderful frost: the photographer's delight. View over the yew garden to the wild garden, yew pillars and the woods, with the wavy beech hedge in the foreground.

to get their plants in fresh from Holland, so the plants are less likely to be pot-bound than in a nursery, where the staff are hard-pressed and short of time. And garden centres sell plants *in flower* if they can, which is the way to buy them unless it's a foliage plant you're after. You can see what you're getting. You can go and look at a border, see exactly what's missing and go shopping. Come back and stick it in and see if it works. If your memory can hold all the way to the garden centre (I no longer take such feats for granted) you should get it right and give yourself, and your garden, instant lift.

Romance entered my imagination after a visit to Elsing Hall in Norfolk. An unforgettable image – two absolutely enormous bells on either side of an entrance to a bridge, flanked by hogweed (this is probably illegal). Wow! Then an ancient timber-framed moated house with a garden full of roses and – the essential and wonderful addition which made the scene – hundreds of purple opium poppies. Everywhere (repetition again).

How to translate such a vision? Well, the poppies are no go. Tried them endlessly and they just don't want to do anything here on the Welsh border. Any of them, even Welsh poppies. How can this be when I love them? My friend, further into Wales, can do it – they look as though they will define her garden, too. I mulch, which might be part of the problem, but oriental poppies don't exactly rave about being here either. And it was the luxuriance and randomness of the poppies that defined the dream. And roses – but they're another story. So the vision stays untranslated and there is one garden I would love to have and never will. And one to remind myself of when I think I could happily go all minimalist and make do with shapes, hedges and grasses.

BOOKS
It is notable that there is not much about plants in my reflections on influential gardens. They were another source of bewilderment to me as I began making the garden – thousands of plants and mostly I would just read about them. This has left me still with an embarrassing habit of mispronouncing plant names, usually because I've never heard them spoken. But I did read about them in books, searching relentlessly for spreaders or seeders. I regarded plants as weapons, the means of covering and keeping the ground once I'd cleared it of turf, and Graham Stuart Thomas's *Plants for Ground Cover* was my bible. And no, I did not go out and hunt them down in nurseries – there was no way I could afford that. If I came across a plant that I knew was especially rampant, ineradicable and mad I might treat myself, especially if I had read lots of warnings about it from garden writers. One of the best was a single plant of variegated ground elder, which after a relatively slow start went on to cover the ground in

the whole of the front garden. Then I also discovered *Lysimachia ciliata* 'Firecracker' and that took off and settled happily into the ground elder, and the two live happily with the larger plants among them, keeping the weeds down, making a stunning combination, especially in the spring, and providing a coherent backdrop to the planting.

With this kind of recklessness you may be amazed to hear that the only regret I have had is that I added vincas (periwinkle) where I no longer want them and am unable to get rid of them. After all, the worst and hardest plant to remove was already here: ivy (and my relationship with that is complex and ambivalent).

But no, I worked my way through *Plants for Ground Cover* searching out their seeds, and for many years the nursery was the powerhouse of the garden. I sowed vast quantities and raised a few – the number that failed to germinate was depressing, but enough did to keep me at it. So I can hardly claim that the garden was designed in the proper way with plants carefully selected for their sites (what luxury . . . or maybe it would be too much to cope with). I planted what I got.

My other source of plants was a friend who was addicted to taking cuttings. I do believe that you'll be a cuttings or seed person by inclination. Seeds always seem to be to be full of promise. I enjoy all the bits of growing them, from seeing the amazing emergence of newborn seedling to all the potting up. I associate cuttings on the other hand with mildew and rotting off and general failure. Anne, however, was a cuttings fiend, forever growing hundreds of new plants and enormously generous with them. We shared whatever we learned about good ground-covering plants and between us grew all we could. Anne helped found the garden.

My other plant bible was Robin Lane Fox's *Better Gardening* and I'd recommend it to any beginning gardener. It is out of print but the wonders of the Internet mean that it is not out of reach. It served the essential function of restricting my range when I was tempted to stray beyond herbaceous ground cover. Here were short lists of each kind of plant (usually ten of each): trees, shrubs, herbaceous and so on. An end to bewilderment, a definitive core garden. Brilliant, and you will find the bones of the Veddw in it. At least those which have survived (shrubs tend to keel over with sudden death in this garden).

Beyond reference books, what did I read for pleasure? I was short of money, remember, and I think there were far fewer garden books being published in my early gardening days anyway. But needs must – I ravenously acquired old garden books from any second-hand bookshop I came across. I had a wonderful time. I have longed for years to introduce some of these books to a wider public, especially since the Internet has made finding old books less of a frustration, but I've been unable to sell the idea of a feature on them to any magazine or newspaper.

In 1912 Constance O'Brien published *The Guild of The Garden Lovers*. One of the strangest things about this book, now nearly a hundred years old, is how contemporary some of the things it discusses are: 'When the really beautiful idea of wild gardening was introduced to the public, it suffered just as much from becoming a fashion as the less admirable forerunners had done.' And 'Much hindrance to this making our gardens our own has been caused by narrowing the proper pleasure to be got from them down to the admiration of the beauty of the flowers, and lately there has been an inclination to think mainly of their colour and how it shall be arranged. Now colour is important to the beauty of a garden but it is not everything. We want to do something more in our gardens than go about merely staring at beautiful objects, as one does at a flower show. We want anticipation and surprise and memory . . .'

Part of the delight of this book is the idea of a group of women friends creating a 'Guild of Garden Lovers' and corresponding with each other about garden problems. I see I paid £1.75 for this treasure. It feels like an early version of Twitter.

I could originally get books by Marion Cran for as little as 75p, but the price crept up as their popularity increased and ultimately I was paying up to £5. These were books which were easy for a novice garden-maker to identify with. Not only were they descriptions of someone doing exactly the same thing as I was attempting to do, but this was at a time (between 1913 and the 1940s) when it was acceptable to digress into personal issues in a garden book, and we learn much about her life. This includes her having to leave her first garden when she divorced the 'Man of Wrath'. Her book titles give the flavour: *The Garden of Ignorance, The Story of my Ruin, The Garden of Experience, Wind Harps*. She became a popular radio broadcaster on programmes such as *Woman's Hour*, a forerunner of Alan Titchmarsh, now largely forgotten, but still able to speak directly to us: 'Half of gardening is self-control. Few garden lovers start off with the instinct to paint bold flowers-scapes. They almost invariably plant a little of everything, to find they have nothing in the end.'

Some books were wonderfully bizarre. Roy Hay was still appearing in garden magazines in my early days, but even then seemed weird: 'Counter-measures [to pigeons] at the moment consist of spraying some plants with quassia extract, others with the alum solution (4oz to the gallon of water) that is so useful for keeping birds from picking the buds off fruit bushes. If these fail we will try a BHC spray, as I am told dogs will not go on a lawn treated with it.'

Of course I also read Gertrude Jekyll. And was intimidated. And because the plant names have all changed so much (and there was no Internet) I didn't understand her planting much. But I understood this:

I am strongly of the opinion that the possession of a quantity of plants, however good the plants may be themselves and however ample their number, does not make a garden; it only makes a collection. Having got the plants, the great thing is to use them with careful selection and definite intention . . . it seems to me the duty we owe to our gardens and to our own bettering in gardens is so to use the plants that they shall form beautiful pictures; and that, while delighting our eyes, they should always be training those eyes to a more exalted criticism; to a state of mind and artistic conscience that will not tolerate bad or careless combination or any sort of misuse of plants, but in which it becomes a point of honour to be always striving for the best. It is just in the way it is done that lies the whole difference between commonplace gardening and gardening that may rightly claim to rank as a fine art.
(Colour Schemes for the Flower Garden)

There were many others, of course. Margery Fish with the unbelievable husband. Vita Sackville-West, whose books were still affordable then. Lots of women, far more than I can mention here.

All that seems rather quaint, however contemporary some of the themes. A long way away, I realize, from the current star-studded scene. A quieter, more domestic world. One very much worth returning to for any impoverished garden beginner. Makes second-hand bookshops totally exciting.

A HISTORY OF THE SITE

We arrived, I began a garden, but I knew no one and I couldn't understand the landscape. I got to work reading and learning all I could to help me make sense of the place and to make myself at home.

There *are* villages in this part of Monmouthshire, but most of them are a function of a twentieth-century planning system which favoured clustering new houses in 'villages' rather than allowing further scattered housing in the countryside. Before those planning decisions a commentator (Dorothy Sylvester, in *The Rural Landscape of the Welsh Borderland*) remarked of Monmouthshire that

The Welsh borderland is rich in names which have mutated regularly and are neither English nor Welsh any more; the numbers here record the dates when these spellings were used.

'Hamlets are rare, villages still more rare, and the majority of parish churches are solitary or associated with only a minor habitation group – a *ty'n llan* [parsonage], a farm and a cottage or two.'

For all its strangeness this is a small world with great resonance and a significant place in our cultural history. A couple of miles down the lane from here, near Tintern Abbey, are the remains of the Angiddy Wireworks. One of the earliest industrial sites in the country, it dates back to 1568 when the Company of Mineral and Battery Works began iron production in the Angiddy valley. The Angiddy valley, now so characteristically quiet and rural, was the site for the first industrial blast furnace in the UK. The river Wye offered transport, the Angiddy Brook water power, and the woods, which still surround the site for many miles, charcoal for fuel. Iron ore had been mined here since before the Romans. The 'cinders' name you'll find locally, as in Cinderhill Street, is related not to a fairy story but to the remnants of ancient smelting furnaces.

Then in the late eighteenth century the Wye Valley helped give birth to another phenomenon: tourism, inspired partly by a new interest in the British 'landscape'. When the Continent was closed for foreign holidays by the Napoleonic Wars, and people were forced, just as many were by the recession of 2009, to stay in the UK, the Wye Valley became a prime destination. It is strange to reflect that what they experienced at Tintern was not the rural peace and charm which makes the Wye Valley popular today:

Here, now no bell calls Monks to morning prayer,
Daws only chaunt their early matins here;
Black forges smoke, and noisy hammers beat . . .
(S. Davis, *Poetical Description of Tintern*)

The tourists explored the Wye Valley by boat – the road which runs alongside (and which today is frequently closed by landslides) is a Victorian addition. They brought along their Claude-glass, the precursor of the now ubiquitous camera. This was a mirror, and its use involved turning your back on the real landscape and viewing prescribed and admired 'views', miniaturized, in the mirror. The interest in the British 'landscape' as 'pictures' is said to have begun with the Reverend William Gilpin. A pioneer of the Picturesque, he saw the landscape as 'expressive of that peculiar beauty which is agreeable in a picture'. The use of the Claude-glass typifies this perspective.

This has tremendous significance for the appreciation not just of landscape but of gardens, where a 'Garden of the Year Award' can be based on viewing slides rather than garden visits.

It seems quite extraordinary to me that anyone can seriously maintain that seeing a set of slides of a garden is a fair communication of the experience of sight, sound, sensation, stimulation, weather and atmosphere that a garden offers, but we can see in the Claude-glass the beginning of the distancing from immediate, immersed experience into inspecting framed views. The ubiquity of the camera then led notoriously to queues of tourists waiting to photograph rather than look at various 'sights'. Have we now moved to a state where a photograph is an entire substitute for experience and the garden-interested no longer feel a need to actually visit a garden?

The Wye Valley tour also included a famous garden at Piercefield, which incorporated this interest in 'views'. The garden offered celebrated viewpoints along the magnificent cliff tops high above the Wye, as well as a grotto, a giant's cave, a druid's temple and other thrills for the tourists, who famously included Wordsworth, Coleridge and the botanist Joseph Banks, who wrote, 'I am more and more convinced that it is far the most beautiful place I ever saw.'

We live a few miles further towards Monmouth, apparently, according to our address, in Devauden, which is actually half a mile away and which was created in the nineteenth century by a pious man called James Davies, who wished to rescue the 'rude, ragged, boisterous mountain children' from their ungodliness. The Duke of Beaufort, who owned most of Monmouthshire, gave him a small patch of land in Devauden to build a church and school on and this brought Devauden into existence as a new village. The process was later completed by the addition of a small council estate in the 1970s, and then a massive private estate in the 1990s.

The cottagers in the Veddw, down the road, were the principal object of James Davies's ministrations: and that's us. Or rather, our predecessors on this site.

As I learnt all this I began to understand the place I was living in better and it became possible to feel more at home. And I was fortunate enough to find some marvellous documents. One James Ashe Gabb wrote an account of Davies' work, 'A Brief Memoir of James Davies: Master of the National School, on Devauden-Hill', with the objective of raising funds for the school. From this I have a wonderfully patronizing description of the people of the Veddw:

> The Fedw is inhabited by wood-colliers, mule drivers and labourers, connected principally with the wireworks of Abby Tintern, or the adjoining woods, who have encroached on the wastelands of the Duke of Beaufort and enjoy by his indulgence their little cottages and gardens unmolested. These habitations have multiplied considerably within the last few years and are a fruitful source of scholars to Devauden School . . . They originally reared

their turf and mud cabins amidst the rocks . . . They subsist chiefly on potatoes and the coarsest kind of bread . . . It was amongst these people, and on this wild heath, that the subject of my memoir took up his abode . . . The benefits which he has conferred on them by his example are very apparent; their wretched huts have gradually been superseded by stone built cottages. . .

The cottagers 'lay in darkness and the shadow of death', 'living without God in the world', 'having minds as uncultivated as their barren hills'.

And the following year Sir Thomas Philips wrote his *Life of James Davies of Devauden* and provided me with more information:

That population consists principally of small farmers, quarrymen, woodcutters and labourers, many of whom have reared their cottages amidst the woods, or upon the commons; and by great toil and perseverance, have cleared the ground from stones, furze and heath. These men hold their cottages and the small enclosures by which they are surrounded, of the Duke of Beaufort, as lord of the manor, at moderate rents, usually on life leases. Accustomed to scanty fare, inured to poverty, suffering occasionally from cold and hunger, and exposed to peculiar temptations, they have been accused of dishonest practices, and of those acts of petty fraud, which often prevail amidst such a population.

It's hard to be clear about this picture of people living here 160 years ago. It's very vivid in its way, but the gulf between them and me is so enormous that my imagination is defeated. However close I may get to a glimpse of their physical world, I can never approach understanding their mental and emotional world. I feel tantalized and frustrated. Hard to believe they were as real as I am – or that I and my world will one day be as lost as theirs is.

It is actually almost as difficult to understand what it was like to live here in the 1950s. There have been two families who lived in this house for long periods of time, decades. The family who probably built the house, the Evanses, lived here throughout the nineteenth century. A generous census-taker told us that in the 1890s Elizabeth Evans lived here and was at that time an agricultural labourer's widow, who 'kept a cow'. Having a cow was the equivalent of a pension, if not a very luxurious one. The cow perhaps not only gave her cheese and milk and possibly calves, but also thereby an income. The cow must have lived in what we grandly call the barn but should more accurately be called the cowshed.

The Evans family stopped living in Veddw House in 1911, though they continued to live in the lane. The family who succeeded them lived here until the 1950s and

I have had the astonishment of having three sisters visit who lived here in the 1950s: two of them were born in the room where I am writing this. The lives they described to me, with the four children, parents and grandparents living in a two-up, two-down cottage, seem almost as strange and distant as those of our nineteenth-century predecessors. Yet, this is in my lifetime.

One of the questions I am frequently asked is 'What does Veddw mean?' It probably means 'birch'. The alternative and less friendly version of this query involves a lecture on how this is not a Welsh spelling, followed by a lecture in how it should correctly be written and pronounced. This is wearing and it overlooks the principal characteristic of this area: we are a border county.

This has influenced the history, language, place names and culture of the area – it is an in-between land where immigrants have settled for thousands of years.

The wild garden with yew columns, *Magnolia stellata* and daffodils providing a background to a memorial stone to a delightful and lost hybrid name of the Welsh/English border. (Memorial stone by Catriona Cartwright.)

Roman soldiers lived and fought here and built towns (their descendants, the Italians, brought their ice cream here in the twentieth century); the Normans built some of their first castles here; and the English and Welsh have mingled forever. The coal-mining industry was made possible by massive immigration. The result is a glorious mix which emerges in delightful place names, mixtures of English and Welsh such as Ffymony Yearll, now Earl's Well and clearly derived from the Welsh for well and the English for earl, and the village with three entrance roads each with a different name on the signs: Trellech, Treleck and Trelleck. You may be sure there are angry people anxious to get rid of this delightful local idiosyncrasy in the interest of uniformity and in turning border into Wales.

Monmouthshire has traditionally claimed to be English, and resentment still lingers among some of the older locals at the way we have been sneaked into Wales. English sentimentality also feeds a desire among more recent immigrants to join with Welsh nationalists and turn Monmouthshire into an uncontaminated Welsh county, to which end our places are rechristened. Christopher Booker, in a recent *Spectator* article, quotes an Indian businessman who pointed out that 'Mumbai, Kolkata and Chennai are only names for the front of buses. We still talk about them as Bombay, Calcutta and Madras.' The same is true of course of the frequently spurious 'Welsh' names here (Cas-gwent for Chepstow), but no one is that relaxed about it. So the highway department insist to me that 'the Fedw' is so named by them on their new sign because that is *Welsh*. They are apparently oblivious to the fact that no one could truly claim 'the' to be Welsh. And so a delightful tradition is inadvertently continued.

Garden visitors often come to me to tell me that Veddw is a misspelling of a Welsh name, which they usually offer as Fedw (a version of the Welsh word *bedwen* – don't ask!)

The notion of a 'correct' spelling is relatively new and most inhabitants of the settlement would have been unlikely to write the name anyway. (Though they might have read it – at one time more people could read than write.) But some people did write it and I have seen these versions in documents: Vedow (1569), Veadow (1763), Fedw (1812), Vedw (1828), Veddw (1929) and Vedda (1947 – still the indigenous locals' pronunciation). I wrote these on one of our benches in the hope of subverting this preoccupation, but in vain.

Of course, all this is very recent history and when I came I had a lot to learn about the more distant past. I had an idea that before the Romans marched past our house (I know . . .) the whole country was covered with forest. Oliver Rackham put me right about that as much else, and I became aware that there is an Iron Age hill fort a couple of miles away that suggests that some kind of farming was going on in the vicinity at the time, to feed whoever and whatever happened in the hill fort. In fact, that this little patch of land, just like the little patch of land you live on, was, if not inhabited, very likely in use since not long after the last ice age. And this gave me an abiding interest in prehistory. Even this has managed to get me into trouble, since studying the Celts leads to the conclusion that there were never any such people living in Wales. This idea is not popular with the Welsh.

But closer to home was my detailed research on the settlement of the Veddw itself. It is truly amazing what it is possible to discover and I would recommend that anyone with an interest in their own site go to the record office and start looking. Good as family trees. Or better.

HELLEBORES

Who could not love the oriental hellebores (*Helleborus* × *hybridus*)? Well, I do feel a little ambivalent about them. Their flowering in winter is perhaps to be grateful for, but do we really want to have to go out into the cold and wet to admire them? When you do you have to stand on your head to see the best bit, which is the inside of the flower, because they tend to hang their heads. Newer varieties, less so, fortunately. And they don't make cut flowers easily, having a depressing tendency to wilt if cut. You can, and I do, cut the flower heads off to float in a bowl, which sounds glamorous but is strangely unsatisfying. And then they sort of sag and fade and, unless they all go at once (unlikely), faded ones have to be fished out. Some people place a mirror under a flowering plant in a pot – but I rather think that shows what we are up against.

And they are susceptible to a depressing black fungus, so get unsightly blotches

Helleborus argutifolius when it was still *H. corsicus* (and unspoilt by fungus).

on their leaves. This leads people to tell us to cut the leaves off in November. I'm not sure why and it doesn't seem to help, but I have to confess I have never been rigorous about it so don't take my word. I'm not sure I like the rather strange look of them without their leaves, standing naked – a bit like meerkats without the cute factor.

They are very solid, substantial-looking plants though, revered in many quarters.

And the number of photographs I take of their flowers suggests I love them really. Oh, well, five out of ten for cheering winter up. A bit.

Helleborus argutifolius is good: seeds generously and its leaves and solid assertive form play something of the same role as hostas. And like hostas it has a fatal flaw – that fungal disease. Always looks worst just as it is coming into flower. I had big plans for this one but have sadly given it up.

But don't forget *Helleborus foetidus*. You can forget worrying about the 'stinking' (*foetidus*) part – not applicable to any use you'll make of it. This sweet, rather background plant has consoled me through dire winters with its well-presented, robust, small bells. In a tiny jar or vase it will last for ages. Sometimes it will behave like a hellebore and droop depressingly when cut but mostly it stays perky. Nearly as good with snowdrops in a vase as the early leaves of *Persicaria campanulata*, which has very early (January) rough tough leaves with a delightful stripe. This hellebore has now got the horrible fungus disease. So scrap this recommendation if you have any evidence of the fungus in your garden.

PLANT OBSESSIVES

I am not endlessly fascinated by plants, which separates me from the many gardeners who live for plants and who would probably be offended by my inclination to see plants as my tools. Worse – when I was desperately covering the ground and attempting to keep weeds at bay, I used to see plants as artillery in the struggle. A good plant was one which would hold its own and then spread, either by seed or by elbowing. People still call me 'brave' for growing certain plants, which are seen as 'thugs', because, presumably, they want space for lots of different plants and will not offer space generously to any particular plant. Which is one reason why there are so many appalling gardens. People describe themselves as 'plantaholics' without any of the shame you'd think such a term should provoke, and 'plantsman' – a kind of cultivar of a plantaholic – is a term of *praise*!

Many people look with private horror at houses full of knickknacks. A garden full of the equivalent leads to lecture tours and media admiration. No wonder the world fails to take gardens seriously. And no wonder, if I see plants as tools, that I am alienated from a vast number of my fellow gardeners. I have spent an evening inspecting a plant collector's garden in the company of such obsessives. I felt like a visitor from outer space, having no idea why these people could get so preoccupied with whether this plant was '*wallenchia*' or 'whatever'. For them it was the *only* way to engage with a garden and any idea of seeing what these plants contributed or failed to contribute to the garden as a whole was incomprehensible. I have as much in common with these people as I have with collectors of pincushions, and I hate the resulting feeling of alienation. And, even more, I hate this, for me, travesty of an approach to a garden. I know people garden-visit for the teas and for the plants, but I long for those who can enjoy a garden for its own sake.

The garden world, as represented in the media, supports the knickknack view of a garden. Any number of those gardens which are publicly lauded and applauded are plant zoos. But nearly every house in this country has a garden. I wonder if there are some gardens out there being made by people who hate gardening, people who would remove an ailing plant rather than nurture it to death and who don't want to collect plants. People making simple, clean-lined, elegant gardens. Such people have no encouragement to consider that they may be making far and away the best gardens. There may be many hidden joys that gardeners will never see.

THE FRONT GARDEN

The front garden is just as it says – at the front, opposite the front door. We pass it every time we go out to the garage, to feed the birds, to go to the dustbin, to greet our visitors, and it is visible from our sitting room, my bedroom (where I live, really) and my office (next place of residence). Every time I sit in mild frustration, waiting for the computer to do something, I look out at the front garden. Important view.

And that is why, if I can find the time and energy, I cut down all the herbaceous plants in the autumn, in defiance of current fashionable practice. It seems that every article published about autumn or winter gardens for the past fifteen years has extolled the virtues of leaving plants to overwinter, to benefit birds and to provide beautiful seed heads. I leave the cuttings *in situ*, making a very effective mulch. And I guess that the seeds the birds could eat if I left them standing are still there for them to find in the herbaceous debris.

All this stuff is partially right. It's well worth hanging on to grasses, especially miscanthus, as they look beautiful all through the winter. Some other plants look good too – but not half as many as we're supposed to think. Don't be persuaded to leave things you'd rather see the back of drooping and dripping all winter.

Anyway, going back to the front garden. I originally thought 'cottage garden'. I thought, like many before me, that it would save me thinking much about plant arrangement and let me shove in anything I fancied. So I did and it became a right old mess, of course, as that always does. So I began to add some shrubs in order to topiarize them and create a bit of form and order. The garden is the classic rectangle, divided satisfactorily, if not very originally, into four with crossed paths. So I added a couple of shrubs in each of the quarters. One of these – wheee! fast growth! – was golden privet (*Lonicera pileata*). What a miserable plant that is! It did grow quite fast but it never gave up shoving up random spindly shoots and it stayed wobbly instead of compacting nicely. I dug them up and was left with four *Osmanthus × burkwoodii*, which also grew quite fast and were entirely satisfactory. More! I thought, pleased with the sight of these sculptural shapes; and so I added box balls down either side of the central path, using whatever box plants I had to hand, that being the necessity then. So they don't match or grow at the same pace. And I then also added some alongside the other cross path, and they haven't made it to size yet. But there they are: very ordinary (apart from lack of uniformity), unoriginal and satisfying.

The front garden, with a view to the meadow through the huge hornbeam tunnel (huge job to cut). Box balls and the larger *Osmanthus* x *burkwoodii* ball give year-round chunkiness. Featuring in high summer, *Euphorbia griffithii* 'Fireglow', *E.* 'Dixter' and *E. cyparissias*, with *Humulus lupulus* 'Aureus' on the fence, all having a shout. Cotinus adds a touch of purple. And *Aegopodium podagraria* 'Variegatum' – yes, variegated ground elder – is losing the battle for space to *Lysimachia ciliata* 'Firecracker'.

They look good all year round, but, of course, come into their own in winter, these clipped shapes. And they are why it's good to cut down the foliage that crowds round them all summer – to show them off better. And it makes for a little less work in the spring.

I notice people refer to this as my 'hot' garden, which for no good reason irritates me. It's because I use bright colours in the flowers, which was once regarded as exciting and very unusual. We are very short of real excitement in the garden world and these little sensations have to be made much of as a result. In this case it was because for a long time pastelly pinks and other laid-back colours were *de rigueur*. Before I left London I applied for a place at a garden design school. I went for a kind of collective interview, where at some point the pastel colour theme was presented to us for admiration. I asked what was to be done if a client wanted bright reds and yellows. Witheringly, the interviewer informed me that she did not believe she could design a garden for such a client. I was not offered a place.

Well, I like 'in your face' – and quiet and tasteful too, as it happens. So this is my 'in your face' garden. Whenever I come home from the Chelsea Flower Show I fall in love with this garden. It's the time of year – and somehow Chelsea never manages to pull off anything quite like it. Probably to do with the demand for lots of different plants at Chelsea – because at this time the front garden is full of just *Euphorbia griffithii* 'Fireglow', *Aegopodium podagraria* 'Variegatum' (variegated ground elder), *Lysimachia ciliata* 'Firecracker' and *Ligularia dentata* 'Desdemona' and 'Othello'. All orange and purple (brown?) with that touch of low-growing white and greenish grey for the ground elder. It looks wonderful for weeks. It'll all die now I've said that.

The mix of the new leaves of the variegated ground elder and purple/brown (purple sounds so much more appealing than brown but I do think brown is probably more accurate) lysimachia, both just a few inches high in late spring, is a wonderful sight all by itself and would make a great ground-cover combination for someone brave. If they were grown just by themselves it would be easy to cut them down when the ground elder was coming up to flower. They will then grow fresh new leaves and look wonderful all over again. Good trick.

Later *Crocosmia* 'Lucifer' comes out scarlet: a rare and valuable colour in herbaceous perennials. There is lots of strong yellow to go with it and it all sings again, before fading into a bit of an anticlimax in late summer. There's only so much you can do with one bit of garden, and the quiet clipped shapes will do for the rest – together with the snowdrops which pop out in spring. If you can bear to go for effect instead of a plant collection I commend this planting to you.

A view over the front garden, focused on the trite but well used bird bath, in a frame of box and osmanthus balls, euphorbias, humulus, cotinus, variegated ground elder and lysimachia.

AUTUMN SUNSHINE

It's been a golden autumn. I don't mean by that that we've had wonderful autumn colour: so far, and it's the end of October (2006), we've had no real frost and the only things that have turned must be naturally programmed to do that whatever the weather. The brightness has been brought by the sunshine: even the wet days have often had sunshine in between. I've frequently got up in the morning and looked out to see shafts of sunlight lighting up the trees in the coppice. I love the sight. The sun's low, and the effect really is golden. It shines through the trees, creating real, visible depth where normally the crescent of background trees looks flat because of the uniformity of the greenness. But now there is just enough change of colour in the leaves for some of them to blaze in the sunshine and light up and glow and suddenly it's all three dimensional.

Sometimes I look out of the window and that ridiculous thing that you think people invent simply for effect actually happens: my jaw drops. Something is unexpectedly lit up, as if someone is pointing it out with a spotlight. And it looks so radiant because soft yellow is the colour of the slightly fading leaves everywhere. Not dramatic reds, purples and vivid yellow, just the beginning of turning, a touch of variation from the relentless green of summer, and the sun suddenly points a finger at it and I gawp.

This year I've been chasing it with my camera, sometimes just opening the window and snapping. But there's too much dying stuff in the foreground. The crescent border still looks great to the eye, with the circle of trees offering a backdrop. But frame it in a picture and it just looks a mess. The contrast between photographs and the reality of looking at the garden defeats me – I'm never quite sure why some things look better in the flesh and others in photographs. A photograph is framed and pre-selected for us, so in the case of the crescent border, for example, the whole of it, messy or otherwise, is put before us like pudding on a plate. The eye in a garden roams, unconstrained by a frame, and characteristically goes on scanning, selecting, considering.

Ah – but, it does that surely also *within* the photograph? Hum. Stalemate?

So in a way I've been conducting a love affair; chasing elusive images, trying to capture the enchantment of golden sun and garden. While at the same time people ask me 'how's the garden?' – dreadful question. And I actually want to say 'don't know, don't care.' Because the bit I'm avoiding thinking about is anything that needs doing out there. The grass is growing relentlessly and needs mowing. No joy in that – the mower may make skid marks everywhere and the mower leaves wet little piles of cut grass behind, making the grass look worse than when I started unless I drive over and over it, picking up.

I'm avoiding planting the few bulbs I got this year, because they need planting in the beds. Planting in the meadow is not so bad: you get nice whole lumps of turf out with the planter and the only cost is bending down to pick up the lumps after dropping the bulbs in, in order to pop them back. In beds where the soil is both wet and soft the ground just crumbles and falls back in the hole. Hopeless. Hate it.

Then there are lots of things needing planting or moving – hard work, in other words. Hard work in mud and wind chill. Don't want to think about it. Why do people talk as if I would want to? Best to take pictures. Or write about it from indoors.

Today Charles has gone out there at last with his cameras, because there was a hard frost last night – the first this year – and a good frost always brings out the photographers. Maybe he'll be able to do it: to make permanent poetry out of the combination of dazzling beauty and collapsing foliage.

TRUTH AND THE GARDEN WORLD

The garden world is soaked in dishonesty of all kinds, a dishonesty I seem to find very hard to cope with. I am not sure why this is such a great problem for me when it just simply isn't for other people.

The talking up of gardens in glossy magazines is an example. Now, shouldn't I feel slightly foolish for caring about that? What are glossy magazines for if not fluffy writing, souped-up pictures and expensive adverts? Who on earth takes all that seriously? It appears we're not supposed to and when I have indicated that I thought we might take it seriously, I have ended up feeling silly and naïve.

But – are you sure you've never been influenced by a glossy girlie magazine saying this, that or the other make-up is good? If a glossy food magazine recommends a new product do you assume it's dishonest rubbish or do you take note? None of us has any idea of the motives of the writer in making such recommendations, but I bet a lot of us never even question them. So if a garden is described in a glossy garden magazine as if it were the destination of a lifetime, do you take it seriously?

Well, you're not supposed to take any of it seriously and you would be gravely mistaken if you did. It's a game garden writers play – and, worse, I'm not sure if any of them reflect on it at all. I only reflected on it when I stepped out of line and found bits of my prose disappearing under the sub-editors' pens.

Note the term that garden writers and editors use: 'story'. You'll get a story about how the owners came to own the garden. A trip round the garden – it has one of these and one of those and then you go here and then you go there . . . and so on and so on. Then a few familiar hints about gardening and you have a 'garden story' – and the stories and the gardens are all indistinguishable.

Maybe we can come to terms with this – it's all frippery, stuff to be read in the bath. But newspapers are not magazines, though they may contain magazines. They have serious, adult content too. However, that is not where garden pieces appear. Remember when you were little and the newspaper had a children's bit that was handed out to you when the paper arrived? The bit with puzzles and strip cartoons? Well, it's as if the garden section is intended to be handed out in the same manner to the mentally challenged 'woman of the house'. Probably of middle age, but hopefully spending time with the kiddies, who are also supposed to garden.

So why do the newspapers dumb gardens down too? Well, I am told that most believe that their readers like familiarity and subjects they can 'identify' with. Editors like their writers to be known to them and known to be reliable – copy the right length, not needing much editing – in other words, experienced (read 'well-known') writers writing on familiar subjects. This avoids the risk of having to find money for a 'kill fee' if the piece turns out to be unusable.

Garden editors don't necessarily know their subject – they may be covering several sections of the paper (or magazine). So they go for writers with a track record, who write 'safe' pieces. Reliable. (Boring.) And, regrettably, these writers do not always know gardening from the ground up. This shows in sloppy recommendations and advice. It's likely that the sloppy advice has been well aired for many years in many places and so looks authentic. Editors like to be able to point out to their advertisers that they are offering the 'right' subject matter and recognizable names – it's about branding. And probably no one on the paper is interested in the least in what goes on in the gardening bit. (Yawn.)

Then there is the fear of libel, which is not surprising, perhaps, in a country where you are guilty of libel until you can prove your innocence, and 'defaming' someone can land you in court. That fear has comstrained the freedom of comment in this book. The other universal garden world constraint that has informed this book is the need to avoid upsetting or hurting people. The garden world is small, people tend to know one another, and so it seems necessary to avoid confronting their weaknesses.

We might think that these things may be as true of the worlds of politics, journalism or the arts, but if they were our press would be as constrained as China's, and I rather believe that is not the case. You will not find anything like this in garden writing:

Also, as I discovered when I criticized Zimerman in a blog post recently, some of his fans can be as nasty as he is, and I don't want to pass up the opportunity to annoy them again.
(Damian Thompson, *Spectator*, 6 November 2010, chosen at random)

This is the freedom of the classical music world. Somehow we also have restaurant and arts critics who appear unconstrained by the fear of upsetting people. I do not really know why the garden world is uniquely self-censoring, but it does mean that I cannot be as straightforward as I would wish. I find this painful and frequently find myself in trouble. I can see what I'm supposed to accept, and turn myself into, but I never quite have. Try as I might to avoid it, I tread on toes.

But for a long time I did think that garden writers visited the gardens they wrote up, even if they wrote 'stories' about them. Then a colleague rang up to ask about a garden she was writing about but unable to visit, and cheerfully declared she would be doing one of her 'telephone interviews'. I didn't take that too seriously, until I discovered that I was expected myself to write about gardens I was only able to see in winter as if I'd seen them in summer. And then I read Robin Lane Fox praising Little Sparta very eloquently while also admitting he hadn't visited it. I was beginning to get disillusioned.

And as our garden began to get a name for itself I also began to notice that people would discuss the Veddw, have opinions about it and *write about it* without ever crossing the Severn Bridge. We have appeared in and been praised by reputable newspapers and in at least two or three books, written up by people who at most did a telephone interview and sometimes did less.

Our worst fears about digital photography have also been realized. It has always been the case that pictures cannot replace visits to gardens to give any real sense of a place or communicate what it is like to be there. Which is why we might wish that garden writers would visit, as words help to communicate those things that the pictures cannot reach. But photographs can help us picture a garden and can illustrate some – specific – aspects.

Before digital photography, photographers using film did do a certain amount of enhancing. One well-known photographer was notorious for his unbelievable blue skies. They became a kind of trade mark. And it is also true that photographers flatter gardens routinely. It's what editors expect. But digital photography offers a whole new world.

When digital photography first arrived I remember considerable discussion in the media about how would we tell truth from fiction, but it's a debate that has been strangely silent since digital became ubiquitous. And your pictures of gardens in books, newspaper and magazines are all to varying degrees tinkered with. Not just a matter of the kind of fiddle you are familiar with yourself on Picassa – enhancing the colour or the sharpness. No, bits of the picture that don't look good – television aerials, drainpipes, weeds – are routinely removed by photographers before the images are sold on to the media. Modifications can be drastic.

So it was with a sinking heart that I read about the Garden of the Year Award in *Gardens Illustrated* (December 2009): 'Our prestigious annual award recognizes an outstanding garden that captures the spirit of the garden world . . . The judges each nominate a garden before agreeing on a winner . . . ' This is a prize for a garden, not for garden photography. So how do they pick the winner? They all go and look at the gardens, possibly twice, to ensure that they see a range of what they have to offer? No – 'Each championed their own choice with a slide presentation.'

The other dimension of the lack of straightforwardness is in the garden guides that bring people to gardens. We'll draw a veil over the sentimental lack of discernment in many *Good Gardens Guide* inspectors, though it must be said that the plethora of inspectors, all paid next to nothing, leads to very uneven results. Wales, with my husband, Charles Hawes, and colleague Stephen Anderton, is blessed with severer critics than the rest of the UK, possibly to the overall cost of gardens in Wales. Shockingly, personal animosity has been known to influence whether gardens are actually given entries in one of these garden guides.

But most people come via the *Yellow Book* of the National Gardens Scheme and believe those slippery entries written by the garden owners. I like to quote someone else in ours, which at least clarifies who's saying it.

Presumably, some of that is to do with a laxity in the world in general: I have no real idea. But I do believe this kind of denial also belongs to the locked determination on the part of the garden media and, it has to be said, their clientele, to keep gardens and the garden 'world' *nice*. It is, as Hugo Rifkind said in the *Spectator*, on a different topic, 'The moral dictation of idiots. It's the way that certain topics become unmentionable, not because you'll be jailed for saying the wrong thing, but because saying anything at all will spark a deafening and indignant squawking from a horde of people who haven't really been listening.'

Gardens confront us inexorably with the relentless passage of time, as the flowers come and go in a parade that gains in speed as year passes year. Gardens are in endless, remorseless change and are always confronting us with our race towards death. Historic gardens remind us that garden-makers like ourselves made a garden and then had to let go, die, and that the garden continued cheerfully without them. Is this what is beneath the insistent upbeat jolliness of the garden world? Is this what we conspire to avoid contemplating?

If so, this is everyone's loss, as James Golden recently pointed out in his blog, 'View from Federal Twist':

Death and Happy Talk
A dreary few days of rain is doing its bit to spoil what's left of melancholy autumn. The sun will certainly come out again and play across the dying garden, reviving opportunity for more uplifting views of autumn brew shot through with glittering shafts of light. But all that's left in my cold, wet clearing in the woods will be the textures and foliage colors of a flowerless season – quite unlike the late show of Garden Bloggers' Bloom Day.

Frankly, I tire of the pretty pictures and happy talk so prevalent among American garden blogs; I think this has more to do with American culture and its denial of the facts of life (of sex, death, suffering, rot and dissolution, take your pick) than with gardens or gardening, which can be and often are routes to deeper understanding of our place in this universe.

The focus of American culture on the frothy and the superficial, even the seeking after 'sustainability,' which has long ago been co-opted as yet another commodity, as has 'organic,' doesn't cure cancer, stop wars, end child slavery or work to prevent any of the many other horrors we wish to hide from our eyes. In spite of our diversions, we all ultimately find a path to realization of our own physical end. It's considered bad taste to write about sadness or the darker side of life, though that seems appropriate to our time.

A first step to taking gardens seriously is to allow in the full range of human emotions. Until we begin to do that, gardens will continue to be relegated to the 'hobby' category by the cataloguers of our lives.

Personally, I believe that we owe it to our gardens, our plants, our fellow gardeners and perhaps also to the wider world, to confront this dreadful miasma in all its forms. It not only leads to dishonesty, it is an attitude which can lead to illness and depression. I'm quite good at it myself – the tendency when something awful happens to 'look on the bright side'. We give it a very positive press and encourage it in children and also afflicted adults. Someone dies and we choose to talk about how they'd 'had a good innings' or how they 'went the way they would have wished to' – good ways of avoiding contemplating the stark and horrendous fact that this person has now gone for ever, possibly without even saying goodbye. It is clear how such attempts to cheer ourselves up are also an avoidance of the pain of expressed grief and the embarrassment that that is supposed to create in those around us. In fact, with such denial we also prevent our fellow mourners from comforting us in our grief, reducing them to sharing banalities.

The garden may seem a long way away from such pain, but it is a hard taskmaster. It is as near as we come now to the struggle our predecessors had to wrench a living from the land. It throws the remorselessness of time in our faces, depicting in its endless, indifferent moving on, growing and dying, just how we are fated. There is grief and struggle and real love out there. Forget 'passion' – that is the ephemeral enthusiasm which belongs in the beginning. Mature love encompasses a great deal more than that – survival, scares and scars.

THE MEADOW

The current mood is doom laden. I have just read a suggestion – by a garden designer – that we should convert our gardens to vegetable production to save us from imminent starvation. As a person who'll believe every scare story and who's been consistently frightened for the last fifty years – though by a strange variety of different scary things – I'm prepared to believe we should. But not prepared to do it. It means I have to envisage our garden reverting to the way it was 160 years ago – ploughed up for the sake of growing food. The tithe map of 1841 for the Veddw shows most of our land as 'arable'.

I believe that was the last time it was ploughed, so that those bits we haven't gardened are now old grassland. In the context of a far too busy garden, full of incident and flower, we need quiet, open spaces. We have three of these, based on the original grassland. The principal one is the meadow, which offers an ideal regime because when the garden is low in incident and flower it is flowering its head off. Then it shuts up for the rest of the year. In other words, a meadow is an ideal place for us to plant bulbs – which hopefully create minimal disturbance for

Our meadow with standards of clipped Turkish hazel (*Corylus colurna*) surrounded by weeds (wild flowers).

the grassland. The grassland has its own flowering contribution, in the form of orchids and cowslips – the latter initially encouraged with additions – which spread every year and make us feel we must be doing something good. I have also, fashionably, added yellow rattle, a meadow parasite which is said to reduce the vigour of grasses. This is for our own benefit as mowing the meadow is an annual major anxiety.

Initially we mowed it with an Allen scythe, a wonderful piece of equipment which convinces the user that they have returned to the early days of agricultural machinery simply by its solid, heavy unwieldiness. It had big teeth on the front and enormous wheels and Charles behind it. He shoved it around, chopping down the long grass with these vicious teeth. My job was coming after, raking the grass up and removing it. Both were dreadful, tiring, boring jobs – but one up on real scything, I bet.

It was and always has been, though, an invaluable exchange. I think elsewhere I said that I don't feed the garden. And it's true that I use very little chemical fertilizer, not so much from conviction as from laziness and meanness. We've got a lot of plants to feed (and it is true that feeding plants makes them more likely to grow tall and fall over). But I do mulch for England. It's my religion. And the amount of mulch you get from an area the size of our meadow is considerable. But it does mean that all that hay had to be not only collected but moved.

Various parts of the garden have benefited from this munificence but perhaps none more so than the apple trees, because they're nearest. I wish I could say they have thrived on it.

Our apple crops are erratic and the apples variable in eating quality – so that I have wondered whether my sentimental and unthinking policy of using old varieties has misfired, since the best producer has been 'Acme', from 1944. Older ones, with wonderful romantic names like 'D'Arcy Spice', from 1785, or 'Ashmead's Kernel', also from the 1700s, have hardly fruited and then have produced tiny efforts not worth bothering with. But we may be to blame as non-pruners. Because 'Acme' did us so well – a lovely apple to eat, crisp, tasty, moist and an excellent keeper – we hardly bothered about the poor performance of the rest except to be rude about them occasionally. Now we're paying, because global warming or lack of attention seems to be making 'Acme' rather discouraged, and this year's apples are tiny. It's maybe sulking because the apples it did produce last year rotted in store because we paid them too little attention. (And this year – 2009 – it fell over. But fruited again.)

When I say we paid them too little attention I don't mean we had them out on racks for the mice to enjoy and for us to turn and examine weekly. I still see people recommending this kind of treatment: people so love to be nineteenth

Hazel standards, cowslips and *Camassia leichtlinii* 'Caerulea', in the meadow.

century in their gardening. They'd hardly recommend cooking over an open fire or ironing with a flat iron, but gardening is different for some reason. We had loads of successful apple keeping by the method of filling a large freezer bag with sound apples, pricking the sealed bag then with tiny holes – as in pin holes – and hanging them up in the garage, out of reach of mice. Last year we failed to remove rotten ones, in spite of being able to see them, and paid the price – it is wise to remove them immediately because rot soon spreads in the bag.

I made another mistake in the orchard, perhaps worth mentioning. I planted the trees somewhat haphazardly. I never thought twice about it. Must have had notions about rural randomness. Now, of course, it's really difficult to mow between them. If they'd been in straight rows – oh, bliss.

The mowing is now at least done with a ride-on, which is measure of our success in reducing the fertility of the meadow, the holy grail of meadow owners. As fertility reduces so does the coarseness of the vegetation, and so it becomes mowable. This has the great advantage of being able to mow, take the grass off and move it, all while sitting down. Just my stuff. Sounds a lot easier than the Allen scythe and it is. But it's no doddle. In fact it's often scary as hell. I have arranged for myself to be run over by the ride-on before now – good job I'd switched the blade off, and lucky that at the time it was possible to switch the blade off. (These fancy adjustments seem to decide to stop functioning now and then.)

Things are safer these days: the current model, though still second-hand, switches the engine off when you get off the seat. But it's hardly female user friendly, and in my experience no garden machine of any bottle is. They are all designed for men and far too big. I clutch the strimmer halfway down a shaft which is far too long, with the result that the engine, tucked in my neck, burns holes in me. I cannot empty the grass from the ride-on without putting the brake on so that I can turn round completely and get a grip of the lever – which you're kind of supposed to be able to pull with one hand from a sitting position. Arms too short, of course.

Part of the problem with ride-ons, of course, is that they're designed for people with large flat lawns to drive round and round on, humming away to their iPods. Whatever I get up to – hills and long grass and trying to go backwards or turn corners on wet grass and the rest – is not what it was designed for.

UPDATE: Since I wrote this, necessity (frequent breakdowns just before garden openings) has compelled purchase of brand new ride-on. Four-wheel drive. Is this the brave new world of my dreams? For now the ground is too sodden, after a sopping wet year, and I'm too garden-averse in November, to try it after one triumphantly successful circuit. Fingers are crossed. Whether it will tolerate the meadow – see below – we will not know until next August.)

When we buy, we bring the sellers of these machines – if they will come (not usually) – to have a look and say if their machine will cut the meadow and the rest of the long grass. This produces lots of teeth-sucking and muttering and assurances that this cannot be guaranteed, and is probably unlikely. (Yet we know it's possible because – with difficulty – we do it.) So I do these jobs always feeling that I'm torturing my machine, that its habit of dumping little piles of grass behind it like an incontinent cow is just what I deserve, and that when, as I have to several times a day, I must lie down and reach under the cutter deck with my mitt to scrape off the accumulated mud and grass, what do I expect when I'm using it to cut *long* grass????

One important thing for anyone who cuts grass in these less than ideal conditions – and I've known one or two women who do – is to get a mower which brushes the grass up rather than sucks it. You can tell – the ones that suck have the grass collector riding high in the air. Unrealistic, that. The joy of the brush collecting is that it's like a sweeper. You can cut your hedge on to the grass and mow up the lot as a vacuum cleaner would indoors. It sweeps up leaves as well, leaving all those leaf blowers looking silly, and you can take the leaves/grass/hedge clippings off to a handy border and put them on as mulch.

BULBS

Conventional wisdom dictates that the smaller daffodils are used in situations like this – in fact, anywhere, except possibly municipal roundabouts. For once conventional wisdom is right, especially in an area the size of our meadow. They are in scale and look appropriate – and pretty. They go over without creating an eyesore – no need to go round deadheading, as I've heard some garden writers and head gardeners (what it is to have labour – and waste it) advise. How will you get them seeding if you do this? Maybe the head-cutters' idea is to prevent seeding? Could be, I suppose.

Do they seed? I have no idea. Some of them spread vigorously, but it could be by the bulbs growing little bulbs, as they do. Daffodils flower at different times, so best to have several varieties. I grow *Narcissus pseudonarcissus* (Lent lily), *N. obvallaris* (Tenby daffodil), *N.* 'Canaliculatus', *N.* 'Charity May', *N.* 'February Gold', *N.* 'February Silver', *N.* 'Jack Snipe', *N.* 'Little Witch', *N.* 'Tête-à-tête', *N.* 'Jenny' and *N.* 'Thalia'.

I think. I wish I could tell you which are best or which spread most enthusiastically, but the truth is that I don't know which are which. To identify them when they are in flower would mean going out there with a reference book or a laptop, finding pictures of the daffodils I'm supposed to have and then comparing them with the ones I can see in the meadow. I don't do this. I just like looking at them.

Or do I? Well, yes, obviously I do. But then – and isn't there always a 'but then'? – I minge to myself about how I've not got them, as it were, arranged well enough. The ideal would be natural-looking clumps evenly – but not too evenly – spread across the meadow. It's never been like this. For a start, they all initially come up singly, separated from their companions by quite a distance. An artificial-looking distance. I was totally unprepared for this and it took me a little while to work out what made them look odd and decidedly less yummy than I expected. It was this sticking up on their own – just as I had planted them, of course. A friend had a field of naturalized native daffodils. They didn't look like this. They were packed pretty solid, but even where not so solid they grew in little clumps. It looked like several flowers growing from the same base. This is the effect of time – of those little bulbs growing out of the side of the original bulb. It's what you expect them to look like.

So now, when I plant more, I plant them in little close groups, to replicate this effect. It does look better. I do not, as we are so often advised, throw them around. This would lose me these little groups and would probably do the bulbs no good at all. And, besides, you then have to go around picking them up again in order to plant them. Mad. It doesn't seem to be a problem to spread them around randomly. Straight lines take care and calculation (and then never work for me anyway as they mysteriously develop curves or wiggles). Whether they then look natural once they've grown and started to do their own thing is something else entirely.

It's not just the singleness of new ones. It's the way that in some places they've bulked up like mad, whereas in others they're still a bit sparse. And the bulked-up clumps are not, themselves, nicely and evenly arranged. And then, maybe the grass is too short? Too much leaf showing? Too natural-looking, I say, not aesthetic enough.

I've never heard any of these complaints from anyone else about their bulbs but I always manage to find fault with the meadow. And everything, probably, for which I have some responsibility. At least our daffodils are not arranged in those terrible clumps that are clearly designed for mowing round. Nor do we mow around them – I mow round the outside of the whole meadow and let the grass grow on. The growing of daffodils leads to a lot of remarkably unpleasant sights, though we do see less of the leaves tied into little knots than we used to. Don't ask me why but people used to seem to believe that daffodils liked having their leaves knotted. Our witlessness is sometimes beyond belief. Funny how the nations' favourites – daffodils and roses – produce so much ugliness.

At first the meadow has blue in it as well as yellow and even white daffodils. The blue comes from the crocuses – and I grow big fat cultivated ones as well as delicate species ones. I know that's very tasteless, but big fat cultivated crocuses are not really so very big and fat. I'm never quite sure about crocuses, though usually glad to see them. They only open in the sun – and until they do open they look very, well, nothing much, really, especially the delicate species ones. But they start early, in February, and we need flowers in February. And I have a personal attachment to the species crocuses related to the first days of my affair with Charles, for which reason I always know when to expect them and always see them with thoughtfulness.

So we get a multicoloured, blue, white and yellow theme to start with in the meadow (and the distribution of the colours is, of course, not at all what one might wish . . .). Then the crocuses vanish, the daffodils hit their stride and the meadow becomes yellow and green and that's good. Refreshing after that joyful muddle.

Soon after that wild anemones, fritillaries, bluebells, cowslips, orchids, daisies, dandelions and camassias follow. I grow the big white (*Camassia leichtlinii* 'Alba') and big blue camassias (*C. leichtlinii* Caerulea Group) but also the little ones (*C. quamash*), which come just after the bluebells and look so very like bluebells. The bluebells and *Anemone nemerosa*, our native wild wood anemone, are thriving and spreading in the meadow and clearly love the regime. These I didn't plant, but as woodland edge plants they clearly belong here and no doubt found their own way here many, many years ago.

After the camassias it becomes true native grassland, in so far as it ceases to have much flower and people refer to it as a wildflower meadow. Now that it has had years of grass removal the grasses that grow there look beautiful in a quiet way, and at this point too the meadow takes its summer place as a space of calm, of sun and shadow and of peace in a flowery garden.

The regime is simple and, when the machines work well (rarely), easy. (A wet year just about reduced me to tears – and then a new mower . . .) I mow all the grass off in late July or early August – whenever the first dry spell is at about that time; or whenever Charles gives permission, since he is always sad to see it go and so can delay the cut with his reluctance. It is a joy when it is done, however, because suddenly the space is spacious and open once again, and the view of the hydrangeas and pink *Persicaria campanulata* suddenly emerges. And I am looking at a large job done, which is a satisfaction of its own.

About six weeks later it will need doing again, and time begins to press. There may be bulbs to plant, in which case the shorter the grass the better. And there will also come a point when it is too late for the second cut. I have discovered this to my cost. If I am not careful the first daffodils come up with their leaves chopped off at the ends. This is in spite of the fact that I will have carefully examined the turf for signs of bulb growth before I cut. No sign of leaf – but come spring, chopped ends. Bizarre. And it creates a garden pressure, of which there are very many. I hate pressure and this adds another mystery, about why I ever got into this and whatever keeps me going. It isn't a love of weeding.

The fact that the nature of the meadow has changed over twenty years by being cut regularly suggests that it must have been mostly grazed before our arrival. It certainly shows the effect of fertilizer dramatically. A long time ago I emptied the liquid from our cesspit (don't ask) in the meadow and then for some years the resulting patch of lush green growth reproached me. There's something reassuring about that, though – a demonstration that something that we're told about gardens is really true?

I cannot comment on making a new meadow, having never done it. But I do know that some garden writers suggest replacing your lawn with a meadow, or even growing your lawn into a meadow. I think the latter could work and be relatively easy – but it's likely to be a disaster in design terms.

Although a meadow is an open space, giving a visual rest in a garden, and so may appear to have the same function as a lawn, that is where the similarity ends. A lawn, despite notices in public places to the contrary, is for walking on. Or playing, sitting, making love, eating on. Because it has these functions it tends not to be in a good meadow place, as a meadow is not for walking on. Indeed, one would say 'walking in' not 'on' and there is the crux.

A view up the avenue we call Elizabeth's Walk, through a double line of Turkish hazel standards to hydrangeas and the house. This is the moment just after the meadow has been cut: suddenly we have wide-open space and long views.

This is especially the case in a small garden, because the scale is wrong. The sticking-up quality of the grasses will be exaggerated in a small space and seem disproportionally large. Not at all the same thing as a lawn, which by its nature is flat and low. In this context a meadow is more like a flower bed (of perhaps a rather subtle kind) than a lawn substitute.

Equally, where it may be possible that a large garden could be over-endowed with lawn and sitting/eating (and other activities) places, in a small garden the lawn is likely to be central and the place it offers for both activity and visual space essential. Do bear in mind that garden writers don't necessarily *think*.

THE CRESCENT BORDER

The front garden is what we see all year round, as we come and go and look out of the windows. The crescent border is what we see from spring to autumn, when we leave the fireside and use the conservatory. This is one of the best things there is in life – eating there together, just the two of us, or with friends and visitors to the garden. Charles is often away and a sunny evening without supper together in the conservatory always feels like a sad loss.

The crescent border is opposite the conservatory, beyond a narrow border of *Alchemilla mollis* with blue geraniums, and the lawn. I have a friend who finds yellow and blue a very boring colour pairing, but have to say I still love it. The crescent border has an immediate backdrop of a large yew hedge, which in turn is backed, some distance away, by a semicircle of mature oak and beech trees,

No one likes the cut-out buzzards (white here, but now a glowing gold) except us. The view is up the yew walk, where another cut-out – a dove/pigeon – makes a focal point.

creating a perfect setting. The challenge is to create a border which will complement the setting for about seven months. I sometimes think of killing the lot – or getting someone to dig it all out – and plant it with just one, super-effective thing, like my beloved lyme grass. But it keeps nearly making it, and it isn't a great deal of work, and trying keeps me entertained.

We have two cut-out buzzards in the border, subjects of much controversy. Most of our visitors want to get rid of them for a variety of reasons, none of which have yet made much impression on me.

I painted them dark grey at first, not fancying a more accurate brown. But that was dull and they disappeared into the background. So I brought the sky down and painted them blue with grey clouds. Whatever our visitors, eagerly obliging me with their suggestions about what would improve the garden, might say, these buzzards have a particular place in our lives because of a peculiar phenomenon. The left one glows. Long after the sun has gone down and you would think it impossible it reflects light back to us as we sit and drink, and eat and talk – and watch the glow.

The rest of what we look at is more problematic. I have worked, reworked and continue to work this border. Trying endlessly to get it to do good from spring to autumn. It never quite makes it as far as I am concerned. Most of the season it hasn't quite got enough going on. In a good year in early July it suddenly fills up with *Chamerion angustifolium* 'Stahl Rose' followed closely by *Campanula lactiflora* . . . the whole border massed with pink and blue: that is good. Then late summer comes and enough does go on, but it never goes on quite right. I have had a habit of trying something in one half of the border, liking it and then trying to establish a matching pair or pairings in the other half. Where it then won't establish, or just takes too long to have an effect.

Spring brings us one of the very few legacies of the immediately previous owners here – big fat 'King Edward'-type daffodils. They were for many years missing on the far left side, since originally they were growing in grass and something else went on there. Later, when grass had become border, I never fancied plunging into the soggy autumn border, full of enormous plants still in leaf, to plant some more daffodils, just for the balanced picture. But truth to tell it was irritating every year, the way this display of daffodils all down the front of the border stopped too soon. So last year I bit the bullet and got myself muddy and irritated and stuck some in. And it did look better. And after complaining for years about their absence, Charles entirely failed to notice that they had arrived and all was now well. Presumably an irritant removed is simply unremarkable.

Early spring is also when I cut down all the old foliage, either by tramping on it or with my favourite and indispensable tool, a rechargeable hedge cutter. Easier than using a strimmer because I'm closer to the job and am less likely to cut down a shrub. Wonderful tool: I rarely leave the house without it. (Leaving a battery on charge indoors for when it gets enfeebled. Pity we can't do that for ourselves.)

The daffodils go brown rather conspicuously and far too quickly, so that I have to chop their heads off to remove the ugliness: a service the smaller ones in the meadow never require. Pink pokers of *Persicaria bistorta* 'Superba' start the next show, alongside *Thalictrum aquilegiifolium*, which picks up the pale pink/purple colour almost exactly. The persicaria spreads pleasingly – at least it did until the year when it mostly got eaten by a rabbit and I had to start again, establishing it from scratch. It took a long time to recover it into the intended sizable clumps. The thalictrum seeded itself (this must have been before the mulch created from the cut-down border began to get too dense to permit seeding) generously in the border, so that this pairing repeats in a kind of regular, random pattern right across the border. This is the plan: that various different complementary plants will take their turn in this way, set off against a purple berberis (the pair of it at the opposite side is still only eighteen inches tall – one of those prolonged attempts to establish a plant which clearly doesn't really wish to oblige. It is very hard to grow a slow shrub among gigantic herbaceous perennials. It looks fine in spring, but two weeks later it's vanished and swamped.)

Anyway, the pink looks great against the *one* purple berberis, and elsewhere it looks good with the white-striped grass *Phalaris arundinacea* var. *picta* 'Feesey' – better known as gardener's garters; the purple rhubarb *Rheum palmatum*, also not managing to establish well on the left side; and *Hosta* 'Krossa Regal'. A tale hangs on this last.

For years the border looked slightly wrong without my being able to identify just why: until the photographer Andrew Lawson pointed out the universal bittiness of the leaves throughout the border. It needed something fatter and solid as contrast. Though it has to be said, perhaps, that prairie plantings tend not to have this contrast or much variety of height and they can look superb. Have I actually got this diagnosis wrong?

Well, providing contrast of form was part of the point of the buzzards. And so I also introduced the hostas – one of the very best, with long, elegant pointed leaves in a superb grey-green, 'Krossa Regal'. They took years and a lot of care (slug pellets, before you ask) to get to a reasonable size. At which point they developed an unpleasant variegation – irregular stripes of yellow. Indicating that they have a virus. I understand that I am expected to dig them up and burn them. Well, I have done that with a mature holly hedge and Charles and I have done that with some long-nurtured box balls. And I've had enough. They can slowly expire all on their own and meanwhile I will contemplate what to replace them with. I have

The crescent border with a refined rosebay willow herb (*Chamerion angustifolium* 'Stahl Rose') and *Campanula lactiflora* dominating and generally taking over, temporarily.

been offered slight hope: that if I feed them well, barrowloads of compost, they may recover. Will try. I'm not a great feeder of things, though, so the shock may kill them.

I clearly can't rely on the hostas for the big leaf factor, so I've just bought and added four *Fatsia japonica*. Fingers crossed that that will do the necessary. They may do it generously, and are evergreen.

Anyway, until the hostas went yellow they looked great with the pink things. The pink and grey theme is then supposed to be followed by wonderful masses of the deep pink willowherb, *Chamerion angustifolium* 'Stahl Rose' (see above). Last year I began to think it was unbalancing the border by appearing in rather large slabs. This year it put out an odd pink flower on an empty stalk. It has done this before, so that I thought I had lost it – then it reappeared with renewed vigour. Leaves me curious (apprehensive?) to see what it will do next year.

The whole border would have been better and easier if I'd learnt what I've learnt since – and if I could have afforded to do it. I recently had a new border to make and reapplied the lessons which things like the crescent border have taught me. I contemplated the planting over a whole winter, rereading plant books and rejecting ideas. But one thing lodged in my brain: Piet Oudolf's comment that hostas thrive better in dry soil than the usually recommended souped-up, manure-full, shady borders. This new border is very sharply drained and with rather poor soil.

So when I saw some magnificent (and expensive) *Hosta* 'Sum and Substance' in the local garden centre I snapped up three. Then took them home and split each one, to give me three for each side of the border – and a basis for building a planting scheme. More garden centre trips followed – for day lilies, crocosmia and coreopsis: in other words a yellow border, apart from the addition of *Crocosmia* 'Lucifer' to add a splash of scarlet.

So the method is: start with a basic plant, repeated down the border and in scale with the area and context of the border. Then build up around it. I recommend the trip to the garden centre method: go at the time when you want a particular effect then set off to discover what is in leaf or flower and available. If you like it buy it – and in quantity, always remembering the necessary splitting to double your spoils. (Though I must confess I killed a very expensive and beautiful astelia by greedily splitting it and feel bad about it just remembering.)

Shopping as an approach to border building is a little radical for some. When I submitted an article to *The English Garden* magazine once, suggesting this approach and beginning with the line 'The key to keep your border going into late summer is shopping', a sub-editor removed this opener. When I suggested it might attract the readers' attention she told me she preferred to 'lead them in gently'. So as not to disturb their slumbers, I suppose.

Still, shopping has been the way I have tweaked and worked on the border. I simply cannot picture a border in the middle of winter or even after two weeks of summer changes, so it is critical to do it when I can see clearly what is needed and just where. Planting at any time is the great virtue of container-grown plants, and though planting in a drought is asking for trouble, specific watering of the newly planted is not the end of the world and makes sure I keep an eye on whether they're getting eaten by some wild beast.

It always feels terribly indulgent. It feels like a kind of instant gratification even if frequently the new plant is far too small to make its mark. It's *there* and can be imagined in full growth. The obtaining and planting has been done. When it hasn't it feels like another job to be done; once they're in it feels ticked off. I absurdly tend to go and look at new plants like this every day for a week or so, really just to enjoy them.

The crescent border usually manages to do a great finale. Well, the 'usually' is just superstitious. I have micromanaged this for a while now. The problem is the lopsidedness. Two monster miscanthus are flowering away on one side; several struggling to make their mark on the other. Lesson: always plant as you mean to go on. I think this was a result of 'I'll see how they do' – and then in this case the miscanthus became the stars of the late border and indeed of winter, so more had to be got and evenly spaced down the border. And/but why didn't I then get all the *same* one since *M. sinensis* 'Undine' was doing so brilliantly? Greed for variety of course, the downfall of the British gardener.

The best bit of this view in winter may not be the miscanthus. If I remember rightly it may be the hedge behind. To follow the border round while at the same time being straight, the hedge has an extra piece to the left at an angle. This breaks up the symmetry of the backdrop just enough to please me. And always the backdrop to this border is the yew hedge and then the trees behind: a beautiful theatre. How on earth can people enjoy 'island beds' without the framing that a back provides? Every picture needs framing. A thought worth bearing in mind with any 'wild' bits of garden, which need it more than most.

But before we get to winter there is the late summer glory. The satisfaction and pleasure this brings me was definitely based on my shopping technique. The border used to fade quietly and tastefully in shapes of pink, grey, green and buff. Nice but not enough. I saw, one day, that I needed a vital injection of pow at this time of year. I sped down to the Nurtons, at that time my best nursery and run by generous friends (now sadly closed). And there were helianthus. *Just* right. They are a delight, adding exactly the right, bright finish. And big, and vigorous, rising above all the lower, fading plants, some of which are cut down to expose the fresh new flowers. I love doing this – cutting down the front row of fading plants to expose the layer behind – though it is very hard work, cutting a bit, stepping back to see the effect and then a bit more, and so on until there is fresh life in the late July border.

I know people see the world very differently – I mean this literally. Some are able to 'see' how plants will look even when looking at an empty border in the middle of winter. Some people – Pam Lewis of Sticky Wicket is a case in point – can imagine how the colours of plants will work and then put them together miraculously. Some people clearly have no sense of scale or proportion. And some people use hosepipes to make wiggles for their border edges and should be shot. So when I say I cannot see or remember borders accurately if they're not in front of me I do realize that others may possess this skill and don't need shopping. But I offer shopping as the reliable way for those like me.

Be prepared to travel, though. The right plant or plants are not necessarily just half a mile away. And be prepared to look – at your garden. Critically and relentlessly, to see what's missing.

GARDENS AND MEANING

Gardens have a variety of functions, including growing food and other plants, providing a place to play games, offering a retreat from the world (if you're lucky), being a quasi nature reserve – and being a place to give aesthetic and intellectual pleasure.

I spent a great deal of time looking at gardens for television one year. When I thought about them after visiting, the best of them and the worst, I found that they all left me feeling empty. Good as the best were, they remained only decorative. Pretty pictures weren't quite enough for me.

Stephanie Ross says in *What Gardens Mean* that she considers gardens can be art if they evoke strong feelings, make us think, possess formal beauty and stand comparison with the great works of art of the past. That list works for me; though the first two could be either/or: think or feel, perhaps. What I know is that when I first heard that idea, many years ago, it was an exciting revelation. It was a whole new dimension to what I was doing, a new world full of possibility. And I was not in any doubt about what I wanted to explore, since I was researching it all the time when I wasn't making the garden: our local history.

I am not about to pretend that it is easy to express ideas in a garden; nor am I qualified to have a discussion about that here. However, I do think quite a lot about how it fails. I think it fails when it is rendered with a fatal literalism – the 'this equals that' school. You know: these six birch trees are the six wives of Henry VIII. Oh? Why? What, exactly, do they have to do with wives? How do they evoke a wife?

I find myself loathing all those show gardens with 'themes'. I have seen moonlight. It does not look like white flowers. You cannot evoke much feeling either in the showgrounds at Chelsea – unless, perhaps, it is related to what the showground at Chelsea is. At garden festivals like Chaumont in the Loire Valley, the gardens tend to rely on heavy-handed symbolism which requires explanation on little notices at the entrance to the garden. Explanation can support art in all fields, but the art should have its own legs too.

What I have tried to do in the garden at the Veddw is to establish some areas that are a reminder, and acknowledgement of the hard lives lived off this land. What I hope is that the things I've made add to the beauty of the garden as well as perhaps evoking the past. How have I attempted this?

A view to part of the grasses parterre, with the yew gardens and the wavy beech hedge in the foreground. The grass-filled box divisions were based on the 1841 tithe map of the area.

I have added several things: the grasses parterre is certainly the biggest. The pattern of the box hedges filled with ornamental grasses is based on the local tithe map of 1841 and the agricultural landscape which surrounds and is visible from the garden. I like the contrast of the grandeur of 'parterres', made for rich landlords who could afford the luxury of their intensive upkeep, with the fields and their necessary intensive upkeep by the agricultural labourer: I like linking these two disparate and similar things. I like to think it reminds people of the surrounding countryside and its nature, and hope that they see the patterns of the fields in the view from the garden with fresh eyes for having seen a formalized version of them. The fields are still providing food today, so there is another link – the continuities of the use of this land.

I have introduced the low curve of the Monmouthshire hills into the hedges in the garden, for the pleasure of the curve but also because they are different hills from other places' hills and particularize what may otherwise just seem like 'the country'.

I love words, not just as communication but for the look of them. I've used them too. I used them in the cornfield garden, on the rails which contain the small

ABOVE LEFT A view across the grasses parterre to the fields beyond, which the parterre refers to and acknowledges.
ABOVE RIGHT The cornfield garden with the grass *Calamagrostis* x *acutiflora* 'Karl Foerster' contained in railings and box hedges.
OPPOSITE LEFT The cornfield garden rail.
OPPOSITE RIGHT The 'that population' gate – named from the quotation inscribed on it, which was found in a nineteenth-century book, and describes the people who lived in the Veddw at that time.

formal gardens in there. This garden was partly a joke. At the time when I made it there was a fashion for 'wild gardens' and these were usually some sort of imitation small field. I felt for the farmers who would regard their hard-worked fields as anything but wild, so represented 'cornfields' with small, formal rectangular 'fields' – the opposite of 'wild'. These were intended to contain cornfield weeds, but it slowly (I was persistent) became apparent that it is very difficult to grow weeds. They are annuals, so need to be sown after some sort of ploughing (I tried a rake, a hoe, a spade) and the birds ate the seeds, the slugs ate the little plants – and they got swamped by, of course, bigger, unwanted weeds . . .

I have resorted to more grasses just for the look of the thing. The one year we managed to get the poppies, cornflowers, hawkweed and so on they looked fantastic. But so, in a very different way, does the sight of a sea of grasses – *Calamagrostis* × *acutiflora* 'Karl Foerster' – all contained within black rails. On which I stencilled the names of all the weeds and plants I had tried to grow. So they still live there as a kind of ghost.

I have made a gate into the woods, on which I wrote out some of the text about the Devauden School and James Davies. It's always slightly awkward if we go

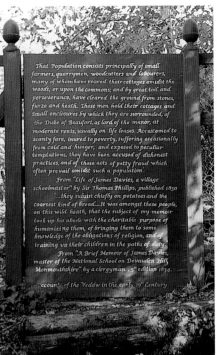

That Population consists principally of small farmers, quarrymen, woodcutters and labourers, many of whom have reared their cottages amidst the woods, or upon the commons; and by great toil and perseverance, have cleared the ground from stones, furze and heath. These men hold their cottages and small enclosures by which they are surrounded, of the Duke of Beaufort, as lord of the manor, at moderate rents, usually on life leases. Accustomed to scanty fare, inured to poverty, suffering occasionally from cold and hunger, and exposed to peculiar temptations, they have been accused of dishonest practices, and of those acts of petty fraud which often prevail amidst such a population.

From "Life of James Davies, a village schoolmaster" by Sir Thomas Phillips, published 1850
'...they subsist chiefly on potatoes and the coarsest kind of bread....It was amongst these people, on this wild heath, that the subject of my memoir took up his abode with the charitable purpose of humanizing them, of bringing them to some knowledge of the obligations of religion, and of training up their children in the paths of duty.

From "A Brief Memoir of James Davies, master of the National School on Devauden Hill, Monmouthshire" by a clergyman 5th edition 1834.

...ccount of the Veddw in the early 19th Century

round with people, waiting while they read it, but it seems so necessary and so good to have it in the garden. It is such a vivid reminder of other lives lived out so very differently here.

I have also attempted to memorialize the now dead local names with the headstones in the wild garden. That's partly because many were such 'border' names, with their wonderful mix of Welsh and English, and partly because some of them are just so wonderful to pronounce. Ffymony Yearll, for example – wonderful words!

I have also tried to keep our ornamentation relevant to the Veddw – hence the cut-out wood pigeons, otherwise and more glamorously called doves, and the buzzards.

I think it is quite possible to visit the garden without any of this impinging too much, but I hope it adds texture and helps bring to mind the rich history and hard lives of our predecessors.

APPEARING ON TV

If you're going to be part of a garden programme on television there's one thing you'll know from the start: the subject is not going to be treated in any depth. So what was behind Channel 5's decision to make a competitive garden programme? As far as I can tell it developed from two things. One was a ghastly programme, which apparently was enormously popular, called something like *I've Got Britain's Best Home* – and this was to be the garden version. And Channel 5 briefly had an ambition to take on BBC2 as a garden channel. That ambition and the person whose idea it was didn't last through our filming. The channel was taken over by Macho Man, who subsequently commissioned programmes like *Extreme Fishing* and *Terrifying Lorry Driving*. (That's not a joke – there were such programmes and they still endlessly repeat on obscure TV channels.) From that point our 'pilot' was doomed. Still, it was fun to do and I don't think any of us expected much from it. It may have included, somewhat radically, criticism and evaluation of gardens, but it was all securely encased, if not swamped by, lots of Lawrence Llewellyn-Bowen admiring the gardens with the proud owners. It was great fun to do, though, and brought in some very useful cash.

Everything was unbelievably last minute. Our team was really cobbled together, with Mark Gregory, the Chelsea Gold Medal-winning designer and landscaper, recruited two or three days before filming was scheduled to begin, and throughout the filming the production company were scouring (the south of) the country for gardens to use and begging for suggestions. The title *I've Got Britain's Best Garden* was a joke from the start and a hard joke on the garden owners, especially those whose programmes never even got broadcast: two out of six of the programmes were shoved out of the schedule in favour of football. An especially deadly demand was that the gardens have attractive houses; another that the garden owners be physically presentable and likely to be suitably articulate when interviewed showing the garden to Lawrence. This apparently led to many wasted journeys on the part of the production team and no doubt to many bewildered garden owners.

Worst of all, perhaps, the plan for just how the competition would work was cobbled together over lunch on the last day of filming. This resulted in some quite incongruous pairings of gardens competing with one another. Perhaps the most unfair and upsetting was pitting the remarkably competent and immaculate, if rather dated, Wollerton Old Hall Garden against a contemporary garden made by a lecturer in garden design with benefit of a superb woodland setting. Chalk and cheese absurdly yoked together.

Mostly the dialogue was our own spontaneous utterances cut into sound bites. Three or four hours of fun got boiled down according to other people's priorities into single sentences with hopefully some punch in exchange for analysis. Various bizarre ideas, like the almost inevitable 'garden tips', came and went, not without us first suffering agonies doing the imitation of pruning or whatever while endlessly repeating banal and boring script. I was at least spared tips as my role was to be difficult and stroppy, and difficult and stroppy garden-design tips are not always easily come by or demonstrated.

Amazingly, given how the team was assembled, we were just great together in our designated roles. Laetitia Maklouf, the 'virgin gardener', managed wild syrupy enthusiasm about nearly everything we were presented with, so it was easy enough to argue and bicker with her as we were supposed to do, while Mark surprisingly often had his own acid comments to offer and also provided the sober assessments of the landscaping and use of materials. And sometimes we were totally overcome with giggles.

The garden owners were kept away from us as much as possible, so as not to inhibit our robust responses. They were enormously hospitable and tolerant, and for their pains were put through a dreadful day of being 'judged' on camera and were, like Oscar finalists, supposed to smile through their gnashing teeth. They got the no doubt compensatory pleasure of the company of Lawrence, who zoomed in and out in his chauffer-driven car and who was also kept away from our mundane presence.

We were sometimes spoilt – posh hotels, lunches and refreshments provided, afterwards treated to gifts, three wonderful meals out and an invitation to the spectacular Talkback party at the British Museum. And sometimes crushed – working without any protection in pouring rain, staying in an hotel with bare floorboards and unmentionable things in the beds. None of us escaped without moments of extreme humiliation, which I will gloss over, except perhaps to say it is not pleasant to be asked to wipe your nose so that filming can continue or have microphones threaded through your underwear. And, yes, they really do call 'cut' and 'wrap' and they really do call you the 'talent'.

We worked in our own clothes, there was no make-up offered, and I had the awful experience of having to drag a case full of my clothes up to London for examination by 'the Channel', who then compensated by giving me the most expensive haircut and colour I'd ever had in my life, or am likely to ever have

The Golden Gnome Award for best-ever female television garden presenter. Awarded courtesy of the Wright Garden Consortium.

again. Did it transform me? Sadly not. Or gladly not, because I could never have afforded the upkeep.

The Channel were constantly interfering, dictating, changing their minds and generally pushing their weight about, to the real despair of the production team.

And then they casually put an elegant boot in. The programme sank without trace until it reappeared on YouTube (though, delightfully, you may watch it only if you declare that you are over eighteen), presumably to assume a permanently ghostly existence in cyberspace as a reminder of an entertaining and illuminating summer. And maybe a straw in the wind if the garden media ever wake up and join the adult world, where a garden may be discussed rather than adulated.

And did this impinge on my brilliant career? Indeed it did. I was invited to supper by two of my closest friends and after a lush meal and a private viewing of the programme I was awarded 'The Golden Gnome Award' for the best female television garden presenter! Fame at last!

PERSICARIA CAMPANULATA

Persicaria campanulata Alba Group spreading enthusiastically.

This plant is a real star if we can confront two universal expectations. First, it needs wet and we are told we are about to have droughts and heatwaves. After three years of relentless pouring rain in Wales I'm perhaps permitted to think that I might adjust my planting when this actually occurs rather than in anticipation. And though it acts as a drought warning by wilting, it has survived Welsh drought (less severe than some) without watering or dying. And, second, it's a spreader and no one is supposed to like a spreader. Well, part of my ambition is to persuade people to appreciate spreading plants – the simpler, easier and more beautiful effect produced by some commitment rather than an endless, irritating variety of plants.

It's wonderful: it flowers for months, like a lot of other late plants. The later things flower the more inclined they seem to keep at it. It has two beautiful forms – a white one and a pink one. In winter it starts early with a perky little leaf which sets off snowdrops in a vase a treat: just the right size and classy with it. To plant it somewhere new, which I am always doing, all you need to do is look for a wet spell (no problem there, so far) and pull some up – just like that, by the neck as it were. Don't bother digging a hole; just dump it where you'd like to see it making a big solid wave of flower, or where you'd like to see it weaving in and out among things which might get a little dull late in the year, and pile something mulch-like on top of it   grass cuttings, compost, pile of leaves. That's all. And if you don't like it, it pulls up for disposal just as easily. Comes with either a white or a pink flower. Done.

BUYING PLANTS

I find butchers intimidating. It isn't the dead bodies or even the knives; it's the whole thing about 'cuts' and feeling totally ignorant. When I asked for a lamb shank and had to say, for some reason – you never know quite what you'll be asked and how daft you'll feel – that I wanted it for a stew, the butcher's somewhat belligerent reply 'never heard of that' really didn't help. (It was a great stew, though.) And then there's the bill. You never know what it will be and it's usually a shock. And I never have the bottle to say 'can you chop a bit off then?' Not done, is it?

That's why I've been grateful for supermarkets, even if the meat isn't always very wonderful. You can see what you're getting and you can see how much it costs. I am using a great butcher now whenever I have the time to go (three-quarters of an hour's extra journey and me evil for increasing my carbon bootprint). And I also use nurseries. But they have some of the same problems and require a bit of bottle.

When I first started buying plants I really did my research. I used plants like weapons, hoping they'd rampage away, covering the ground, eating weeds, defying slugs, making me a garden. I couldn't afford hard materials – plants had to do everything (not recommended) and two acres is a lot to cover.

Mostly I looked for the ones which were not hybrids: that way they would be likely to be worthwhile from seed, and Chiltern Seeds would often offer them. Thus were my sophisticated selections made – and the garden was made from those plants that came up in the seed trays. This too is not to be recommended for brilliant design, but is good for the impoverished.

But sometimes it had to be a hybrid and had to be bought. Especially if it was a land-eater, a seeder or a splitter. At that time there were more nurseries nearby than garden centres, and we met more nurseries when on our garden-visiting travels. So I had to bite the bullet.

On arrival at a nursery you have to hope they don't ask what you want: it can save a lot of bending down peering hard to see labels, but you have to pronounce the name. Having derived all my plant knowledge from books I had no idea how to pronounce the Latin. What does the poor nursery person do? Face down the embarrassment straight away and correct you? Or discreetly say it right later in the conversation? Or do as the Queen is reputed to do with her guests and follow the lead offered, however absurd?

Then there's the 'going to find it'. Me, I usually had no idea what it would look like, so if I was expected to join in the search I had a lot of fudging to do and a lot of finding interest in 'that lovely flower over there' to do. Nice helpful nursery people would then chat to me about where I intended to put it, only wishing to contemplate whether it would do well in such a spot. But there was I, terrified I'd sound totally mad with my proposals, if I could remember at all what I wanted it for at that point besides rampaging ground cover.

Like anyone else I loved looking at plants, hunting for plants, and this was my salvation. Any place selling plants with labels on was a godsend: *learn, learn, learn* – names to faces. Garden centres were often the best for this, with the most helpful labels at a useful height and no knowledgeable nursery person to intimidate me. But anywhere helped. *Yellow Book* gardens with their plant stalls, car boot sales, B&Q, they're everywhere when you're looking and know very

little. Growing the things helped too, of course. I vividly remember wandering around the garden looking for somewhere suitable for *Campanula lactiflora*, of which I had many, all crawling out of their seed trays. All I had to go on was the description, since as far as I knew I'd never seen any. So I stuffed them in at the back of the crescent border with little hope of seeing them ever again – they'd been too crowded for too long – and they became stars of the border and a garden favourite. I know quite a bit about them now.

Campanula lactiflora is a plant that shows up the limitations of learning your plants from plants for sale in pots – some never look

Campanula lactiflora – one of the best, easiest and loveliest of plants.

good in pots and so don't show their strengths. Indeed, how could a plant which grows five feet tall show off in a nursery pot? I believe that we probably grow a disproportionate amount of plants which show off well in pots – and that is where nurseries show their strength. Nursery owners tend to be devoted to their plants rather than their sales. They have to be, to do such a job. So they'll grow what is good as well as what looks good. And for that we must be grateful and support them. And not be afraid to be ignorant and ask stupid questions. Hard, but worth it. Some, like Derry Watkins of Special Plants, will even offer you more than information: real ideas about planting and designing with plants. Like getting a really good joint from your butcher – worth the humiliations.

But don't expect to learn your plants from *gardens*. Some people may label and nothing is uglier or demonstrates more clearly the lack of interest in effect and dedication to the bric-a-brac school of gardening. In spring a forest of labels will assault your eyes. In summer they are still naming the bulbs which you can no longer see. If you really don't know your plants you could be in for some very amazing surprises when you grow what you thought was going to be a wonderful hosta and which turns out to be an obscure snowdrop. We all start ignorant – how are you supposed to know whether that's the correct label sitting next to the plant you admire? I have a small collection of mischievous photographs of mislabelled plants. Someone somewhere no doubt has the resulting mistaken plants.

THE WILD GARDEN

I was always a bit unsure about how to proceed, making a garden out of two acres of grassland. The principal problems were how to clear the grass and then how to keep weeds at bay while the plants grew. Oh, and never mind how to get the plants to fill up the spaces.

Mostly the answer was, as ever, mulch. The first time I cleared ground with a mulch was in the proposed (and now defunct) vegetable plot. I grew fed up and overwhelmed by digging in my first year (getting fed up didn't take long). So I dumped the grass cuttings in grave-sized heaps and planted straight through them. I think we grew beans and courgettes successfully and meanwhile the turf underneath rotted down, creating a fertile soil. In the end the whole garden was made like this and I keep wondering whether that fertility would give out, since it was a kind of one-off exercise. I now endeavour to maintain it by more mulching. In fact, I can't bear the look of bare soil. It looks like an invitation to weeds, which it is.

The first difficulty was what mulch, where from? We did get some manure, but it was hard in the getting, what with heavy shovelling and inaccessible stables. We tried sawdust, from a local paper mill, which was fun. We took the trailer in, loaded it up and then got weighed and charged on the way out. It was light to handle, odd in colour – but quickly darkened up. It was the only mulch I've used that actually depleted the nitrogen in the soil. We're always being told that mulches will do this. If it frightens you but also inconveniences you I suggest you ignore it and if your plants go yellow do as I did and dose them with a little lawn fertilizer (it's high in the missing nitrogen). If you are organic, avoid sawdust.

Later, we were for years able to get bark from the local fencing merchant, and then more recently chippings from a tree surgeon. Lucky us. But in the early days, when we needed mulch most, getting it was a terrible problem.

Faced with a slope below a wood which was covered with wood anemones and violets in spring I tried a different tack: planting into the turf. Turf sounds nice – the image is low and springy and so turf is probably a misnomer here. I mean into the rough grass. I started out growing things that Graham Stuart Thomas said in *Perennial Garden Plants* would naturalize in grass. I grew them from seed, all the ones I could get seed for. Things like *Acanthus mollis*, *Eupatorium purpureum*, *Cephalaria gigantea* and the like. The name of the last identifies the subsequent problem: they were far too big. I suppose in the back of my mind was a kind of medieval turf, spangled with small flowers, and I appear to have been rather dim about how to achieve this. So after several years of effort I looked and realized my mistake. I somehow had lost sight of what I'd wanted, but this wasn't it.

All was not lost, in that there is a semicircle of grass enclosed in a rough square. These large plants worked all right in the enclosing bit and some are still there. And the only time I get the spangled look is in spring, when the grass is low, the wood anemones and violets out and I have added small daffodils. Kind of obvious, isn't it? This is spangling time. It's a good idea to go all white with the daffodils ('Thalia' and 'Jenny'). Yellow is everywhere in spring and that's fine, great – it's what spring is about. But a place dedicated to white and general paleness is a refreshing change. Only it doesn't quite work.

It doesn't work because part of the frame is viburnums and magnolias, flowering just at this time – in white with flushes of deep pink. The wood anemones, less conspicuously, go pink as they are going over. The daffodils' white, however, tinges towards yellow and so it's totally wrong. It annoys me, mildly. It would seem mad pedantry to do anything about it. And no one else complains.

After that the grass grows and flowering plants have to be a reasonable size to compete and read in the grass. I guess the medieval turf was scythed – but how did the flowers survive that? Bet they didn't. I think it is a fairy tale. In all those

A beautiful cacophony in the wild garden: principally rosebay willow herb (*Epilobium angustifolium*) and a vigorous crocosmia.

repetitious 'garden quote' compendiums you find Bacon talking about planting up molehills in meadows with thyme and such. Was he mad? How could anyone scythe a meadow full of flowering molehills? And just how big were these molehills to be worthy of planting? Monster moles?

Anyway, the semicircle then needed something a little more in scale, even if flowering meads and molehills are out. And it hasn't been easy finding things that will work in a place like this. The big breakthrough was a gift of crocosmia. Writing about the Veddw in *Gardens Illustrated*, Noel Kingsbury declared that it *didn't* work: 'The planting is not nearly complex enough to evoke a natural habitat' – though it is as near to one as you'll get in the UK, of course – 'or structured enough to be successful as a border.' However, he was looking at it in July, which is its dull period. (Most borders have them, even mine.) He visited once after that in late summer, when the crocosmia was bringing it all together, and (did I detect a slight note of apology?) he remarked on the effectiveness of the masses of orange spikes.

I love those masses of orange spikes. This part of the garden sings at this time of year, when the orange is dominant but pink mallow (*Malva moschata*), purple loosestrife (*Lythrum salicaria*), blue scabious (*Knautia arvensis*) and remnants of blue *Campanula lactiflora* all add slightly cacophonous notes. What makes it work, besides the dominance of crocosmia, is the green background, which means that although there's an edge to the mix (pink and orange) it doesn't hurt. This year I took a critical look and removed the yellow ragwort (*Senecio jacobaea*). It was just a bit too dominant, shouting 'yellow!' at us like that.

I think that this is a very unusual planting: I know of no other like it. I think it's an interesting idea – enhancing grassland with introduced perennials. I am still experimenting to discover what else will work – which principally means survive in the intense competition. Day lilies are used in that kind of context at Chelsea but here they manage only the occasional flower. Which is a pity because they look so good when they do flower here – you get just the odd trumpet (I planted some of the more elegant, pale yellow sort) snuggling in the grass. They look right: hard to define what that means. Is it the delicacy? Flowers here have to be quite small to fit, small and unsophisticated. Having said that, I have martagon lilies (*Lilium martagon*) here and they are out of scale, too big – but weirdly glamorous. I don't know whether they will survive or whether they will shrink as starvation sets in, so we'll see.

This is the kind of detail that is depressing. No one will notice that the martagons are too big. No one will say, 'You should have them out, they're out of scale.' If I contemplate this reality I sink. Does anyone notice? Does anyone care? Be great if they did, though. It would make it all feel worthwhile.

As having a discerning visitor does. And there are some. Sometimes.

EXPERTS

Recently in the *Telegraph* gardening section I read that using wood chippings as a mulch causes nitrogen depletion – and it does this even after being 'left for a year to start rotting down': the reader 'should be aware that as the chippings rot down over subsequent years they will leach nitrogen from the soil.'

The article goes on to declare that the benefits may outweigh this cost and that you could test your soil fertility levels and top up with nitrogen-rich fertilizers such as pelleted poultry or horse manure. Now, I understand that horse manure doesn't have much nitrogen at all (about 2 per cent of dry weight?), especially if mixed with straw bedding, but don't trust me: I haven't personally analysed it.

If the *Telegraph* 'expert' checked she would possibly find lots of 'experts' to back her up. They propagate these ideas among themselves like dandelion seed. I can't quote any authoritative research either but I do know that in many years of using wood bark and wood chippings as mulch I have seen no evidence of this effect. (Sawdust was different – see page 67.)

Claims like this are good for me – it means that wood chippings and bark are not in demand and I can still get them for free or very cheaply (so don't ask me where from either: I'm not after increasing demand and cost). But some of this rather random, 'everybody says' advice distresses me. The very same supplement had another expert offering advice: 'If the soil has been mulched during the summer, remove any remnants to the compost heap and replace with a fresh layer.'

What on earth for? Why remove any organic matter from your soil to the compost heap? For the exercise? Save going to the gym? No explanation. Want to put people off gardening? Seems like it. Who on earth has the time and strength for such esoteric rituals – to which one might add the turning of compost heaps?

My heart sinks at the very mention of an 'expert', especially one from television. Having been one I know just how well equipped they may or may not be for that role. It would certainly be hard to be on television regularly and be any sort of real expert on gardens or gardening. Television is ridiculously demanding of time and travel. Five minutes of finished film can take several hours, with time taken to set up the scene and then weather, noise and giggles interrupting the filming. When I was filming, the rest of my life went on hold for the duration, leaving chaos at home. Filming takes place in the peak gardening season. If you are going to comment on growing a carrot, best to be there to tend it, not rushing off to meet the crew.

What's more a garden professional is expected to attend the RHS shows and comment on them. I only ever seem to manage Chelsea, and sometimes Malvern, because of the demands of the garden. You will be invited to a variety of press jollies: visits to newly opened 'designer gardens', to seed firms to see the latest developments, trade shows, lunches, nurseries – and best to go if you are to keep up and have things to write about. If you are very successful you will raise some much-needed income from taking groups of gardeners on foreign tours, which will have necessitated preparatory visits. If you are getting past it you will be offered cruises. And if you have small children as well, heaven help you!

If you write articles about gardens conscientiously you will need to take time out travelling to the gardens. Hard enough for any garden writer, columnist or commentator; hardest of all for anyone regularly on television.

How does someone become an 'expert'? They will probably have an RHS General Certificate – a horticultural equivalent of an O-level. They may have a nursery or be a head gardener: before giving great weight to their opinions you may wish to check whether that background is relevant to your problems. Recently a garden expert from a national newspaper had her garden turned down by the National Gardens Scheme. You may feel that has little to do with whether she can grow a good cabbage, but it does raise some questions about her judgement of the quality of a garden.

Consider too the age of your expert. Garden experience develops slowly and there is no way to rush it. What is true of one year may not be true of the next. Ten years' consistency can be followed by the totally unexpected. An expert should be suitably diffident. Beware of certainties.

But none of us can garden, especially at the start, without some advice and guidance. The crown imperials in pots were a great success this spring. I had intended to plant them in the garden, but it seemed impossible to discover where I was supposed to put them. I consulted the experts in my library and I was told – 'will take partial shade', 'prefers a sunny well-drained position', 'it grows best in heavy clay soils or in the better loams', 'flowers freely in good soils – avoiding pure chalk, clay and bogs'. I generally pick the advice that I like best, but this time I was defeated and retreated in total confusion to the potting shed to stick them in a pot.

Perhaps the best policy is to have only one reference book, but, one expert or many, the vital thing is to pick the expert carefully. A few years ago I reviewed a book on clematis (*An Illustrated Encyclopedia of Clematis* by Mary Toomey and Everett Leeds). It was so formulaic and comprehensive that you could tell it couldn't be based on personal experience. I am inclined to take seriously a comment that the cultivation of a particular clematis 'requires free-draining soil on the dry side and a sunny aspect' – until I read precisely the same formula applied to a large percentage of all the clematis in the book. So it was also with pruning, 'recommended use' and descriptions: all written to a formula.

Compare this (Christopher Lloyd speaking): 'C. *afoliata,* an untidy grower, usually scrambling over rocks in the wild. Pleasing in flower, it should have a sweet daphne-like scent. Mine didn't.' Who are you going to trust?

Recently a new kind of expert has emerged: the environmentally correct gardener. Anticipating global warming and drought such an expert makes gardens of drought-loving plants without any use of water. And then recommends this practice to others. Drought-loving plants will rot in a wet climate but they will also die of drought if not watered in on planting and while establishing if the weather is dry. Obvious? It seems not.

A good choice of expert – as in Christopher Lloyd – can help you feel you've got a friend and ally alongside you in the great gardening battle; a poor choice can feel very bleak and discouraging. And involve a lot of mulch-removing, digging out of roots or polishing of stainless-steel spades.

It also seems to be a rule of advice-giving that the more authoritative and objective it purports to be, the less helpful it is. Beware writers who never say 'I' or 'me', but speak from some disembodied expertise which you suspect they picked up from some punitive college lecturer in Victorian mode, whose theories were principally based on the idea of keeping potentially idle hands out of the grip of the devil. These are the people who will tell you that to plant a hedge you must 'double dig a strip of ground four feet wide . . . incorporating about one hundredweight of well-rotted farmyard manure into each six to twelve square yards'. When you've finished struggling with the mathematics and ruined your back with the digging, they then hit you in the pocket by demanding that you buy enough hedging plants to put them in one foot apart. When I planted a hedge I was having none of this. Punitive advice provokes my rebellious streak. I decided I might get away with planting my usual way, straight into the turf, with a four-foot spacing between each of the very expensive baby yew seedlings. That hedge was five feet high after just seven years and the individual plants had all linked up nicely.

However, I have friends with professionally planted hedges and four times as many plants in them as they need. Think of the expense. I try to encourage them to remove at least every other plant and have another 'free' hedge but they are usually in such expert awe that they won't. Some professional gardeners still plant in *two* rows, needing a nurseryful of plants which then all have to compete with one another.

The very best trick is to try things and see. Experiment; take risks, particularly if they involve less work. This way innovation arises and innovation is badly needed in the gardening world. If a job seems exasperating, expensive or boring, stop and think whether there might be an easier way. Plants want to grow; they are on your side as long as you are reasonably sensible. If they don't like what you offer, offer them something else quickly and see if that suits better.

Assess the advice you are given as dispassionately as possible and weigh up what this 'expert' really knows, if you can obtain that information. Try and find an expert who is speaking from and not afraid to refer to their own experience. Beware textbook advice and people who can advise on everything, every plant, every garden practice or every plant ailment.

There seems to be comparatively little real research on gardening practice. I haven't researched this, but it is my impression over many years of reading about gardening. And if there was, would it apply universally? So does your 'expert' garden in the same kind of climate/country as you? Christopher Lloyd gardened on clay in the south-east of England – a very different proposition from Wales, not to mention California. Location should always be borne in mind when consulting him.

Or me.

HOSTAS

There is absolutely no point in growing hostas unless you are prepared to kill slugs, and the only sensible way I have found to do that is regular applications of slug pellets. Until the EU ban them. I am also now struggling with a disfiguring virus which adds horrible yellow blotches to otherwise beautiful leaves. With any other plant I would give up at this point (well, apart from box, the absence of which would leave us with no garden). I don't struggle if I can avoid it and growing hostas is a struggle.

But nothing else offers quite what a hosta does in the UK climate while also looking at home here. They have a large, telling leaf – an unusual sight among so many plants with small bitty leaves. The leaves are among the best-looking in the garden world, growing low to the ground where you need them in order for them to work as contrast and complement. You can get enormous leaves, as in the dreadfully named 'Big Daddy' and the amazing and yellow 'Sum and Substance'; you can get elegant long grey leaves – though perhaps too vertical to use as ground cover – in 'Krossa Regal'; and sheer good value in 'Hadspen Blue'.

Hostas are good enough in themselves to stand alone, as well as offering the complementary role, and I grow them that way in the hosta walk at the Veddw.

I suspect, having said all this, that there are, rather like roses, more hostas than are good for hostas. You can get them in all shapes and sizes and I seriously wonder how many are worth growing. And some are definitely more susceptible to slugs than others. Last year I bought an attractive variegated-leaved hosta and put it in a pot beside the front door. I generously slug-pelleted around and kept topping up the slug bait: to no avail. It got lacerated. Whereas it has proved possible to keep slugs off the leathery-leaved ones I grow in the garden, this thinner-leaved hosta was clearly more appetizing than the juiciest slug pellet to the slugs and snails round my door, despite my passing boot.

When people comment on our unholy hostas I have been in the habit of saying that slug pellets work, though not invariably, and that the leathery leaves seem to have less appeal than a slug pellet to a slug. However, I now understand that some leathery leaves in some situations are as good as fish and chips to some slugs – and that someone has a theory that it's a question of *taste*. Now there's research worth doing: do some hostas taste better to a slug than others and if so, which?

ABOVE LEFT *Hosta 'Krossa Regal'*: elegance personified, in grey-blue.
ABOVE RIGHT The hosta walk, with seedheads of *Nectaroscordum siculum* subsp. *bulgaricum*. The nectaroscordum has horrible leaves, the hostas rather ugly stubby flowers. Planted together they acquire each other's strengths.

No use trying to eat them (the hostas, not slugs) ourselves to find out: I expect we have different taste buds.

But slugs or no, growing hostas in pots seems worth trying to me, because they make a big bold statement and offer a good silhouette: just what most plants in pots fail to do. And some people swear by smearing Vaseline round the pot edge . . .

If you wish for the same contrast in leaf form to add some weight and leaf power to your borders without the troublesome hosta you could try bergenias. (They get nibbled by vine weevils instead, but only round the edges, making a kind of decorative effect and giving you a useful indication that you have vine weevils around.) They are not bad but don't quite hit the spot for me, perhaps because they have never grown vigorously enough at the Veddw. The garden at Wyndcliffe Court, St Arvans, not far from here, has bergenias massed round a pool and they look very effective.

THE TERRACE AND THE POOL

I was determined that I would have no planting littering up the space we made next to the conservatory. It is for sitting out round a table in the sunshine and therefore needs clear space where you can move without risk of tripping up or treading on a plant. I did, however, indulge myself with the odd pot, of course, one of which contained a *Stipa tenuissima*.

The terrace is now covered in stipas. And some *Erigeron karvinskianus* have somehow sneaked in. The result is stunning. Beautiful for months. We sit on the lawn.

Well, it's not quite as bad as that. We can and do sit out there, because last year I got ruthless and cleared all of the plants from a sizable area just next to the conservatory (which we then covered with a 'gazebo', which kept the sun off nicely when we had some). With a shovel, gritted teeth and sheer determination I managed to scrape the soil and plants off the flagstones, which they had been rapidly turning into archaeology. Pulled the remainder out of the cracks in the paving and a clear space reappeared. Inspired, I followed this up by creating a clear path to the door nearby, assisted by the fact that our visitors had been ploughing a way through here through most of the summer to get to the bathroom. They enjoy, so they tell me, running their fingers over the soft plumes of the stipa flowers – except, presumably, when it's raining and they get their legs sodden.

The result, though ruthless, was a great improvement – a result ruthlessness often produces in the garden. There were not noticeably fewer grasses – it always feels hard to shed even one plant but when they're there in quantity, who's counting? Effect is what counts. And the contrast between space and plants added punch. Sorted.

Both these plants are self-seeders and look after themselves. We don't benefit much from self-seeding, being conscientious mulchers, so places where we can benefit should be treasured. I tried *Stipa tenuissima* as one of the grasses in the grasses parterre, with very little success because there was no way to encourage it to seed and keep the weeds down around it while it established. And it was happier in paving than it ever was in fertile soil surrounded by mulch. This stipa is a beautiful small grass and should definitely be planted where you can touch it when it flowers.

The erigeron is seen in many gardens in paving cracks and is a wonderful plant for the job. Large areas of paving (ours isn't especially) need something softening and humanizing them, if a pretty daisy flower can be said to be human. I have been trying for some time to get it going too in the edge of the pool next to the terrace, but alchemilla has its sights on those spaces and is tough competition.

The pool itself was our first major project. The terrace is below the rest of the garden – a chest-high retaining wall separates the house, conservatory and terrace from the lawn above. Beyond the lawn is the crescent border and this is what needs to be visible from both the conservatory and the terrace. So planting between the terrace – which is lower than the conservatory – and the crescent border was out. At least, planting with any height was. The answer – the ideal, flat, answer – was water. Charles built it: his first pool and a major feat of engineering. We didn't know much about pool-building. This one has earth on two sides and a wall supporting it on the other two.

Fortunately, as Charles was in the (long – very long) process of building it we had a visit from a real engineer, who pointed out that there would be an enormous weight with all that water bearing on the walls Charles was building and that the walls needed reinforcing. I take pleasure in passing on this useful tip: water is very heavy. (And as a bonus, garden

The pond, with *Alchemilla mollis* and *Erigeron karvinskianus* fighting for the edges. I am not sure the nectaroscordum seedheads add a lot. *Campanula lactiflora* in the background and unknown water lilies in the water.

designer Michael Balston's tip for swimming pools: 'No turds; no alligators.') The answer was double walls and reinforcing with a spare roll of stock fencing (we used to have this kind of thing lying around), with the ends twisted together to make a reinforced circle. The result is still standing sixteen years later.

The double wall permitted us to put a pipe up in-between to create a water spout dripping into a second tiny pool below. This was finished before the rest, so the water was spouting out of the wall when there was still a great big hole behind. Despite the fact that the water was appearing from three-quarters of the way up a freestanding wall, visitors would still ask us if it was a natural spring. Which demonstrates the wonderful possibilities for entertaining the public with fanciful illusions.

I loved this pool for years and have spent a lot of time standing on a square rock which was conveniently situated at the bottom of the wall. Standing on it gives me the height to see into the pool, watching fish, frogs and reflections. The latter probably led me on to the second, reflecting, pool. Despite this pleasure the pool is a headache. It fills obscenely with frogs and toads in the spring, and has dragonflies, newts and irremovable fish and other assorted life. Including, inevitably, blanketweed. And sometimes duckweed. These are not nice and I have not found any totally satisfactory way of removing them. No chemical has ever seemed to make any impression except on my purse. However, one year from spring to early

summer I regularly took a flat rake of the kind used by energetic people for raking up leaves, and pulled out the available blanket weed. Sheer persistence seemed to pay off, because later in the summer it stayed clear of the stuff (while a threatening sprinkling of duckweed appeared instead . . .). But it was one of the wettest summers on record, so, who knows, maybe it was that that did the trick. So it's still a slight worry and not a total delight, despite jolly wildlife and all that stuff.

But it is flat.

Small pool below larger pool on the terrace in July. This shows the blessing Welsh humidity offers to new walls. They look ancient, with self-sown ferns, ivy and toadflax, which arrived and settled in in no time.

TULIPS

Well, these are one very beautiful flower but useless in the garden. I used to try planting them out in the garden but they mostly died. And then the irritating thing is that you can't see which ones have gone to the great tulip field in the sky until they fail to reappear, so planting matching replacements gets impossible. And worse, by the time you come to ordering them you get tempted by something else and you end up with random pop-ups all mixed together. Strangely, the ones which do stay then sometimes seem to stay for ever.

I have one white tulip remaining from a long-ago grand scheme and it won't go away. It appears in the front garden, ruining the effect that the plants there now create at that time. But I keep it for a not very nice reason: it demonstrates to perfection how a plant association can look good close to – we have photographed it just as it could appear in one of those magazine articles, looking ideally placed. Step back and take in the wider border and it

Tulips 'Rococo' and 'Princess Irene', with palms, against the black wall, make the conservatory sing with colour.

sticks up like a sore thumb, shouting out 'bright white' in a border with nothing else like it in sight. (White, being so harsh, is a kind of killer colour.) So because it paints such a good moral to a moralist I grin and leave it.

Then for some years I planted tulips generously in baskets and this was good. I planted them in pots, and then when they flowered I squished the pots into painted baskets of suitable colours and arranged them to maximum effect – round the bird bath, for example. But there weren't many places for this display near the house, so they went also into the veg plot – and I never went to see them except to water and resent them.

So now I plant them in pots in large numbers of complementary colours and bring them into the conservatory when they begin to flower. This is perfect for us, because it is where we begin to sit at that time of year, so they do get properly enjoyed. It is all very well to seek out a flower but it does place a great weight of expectation on it and raises a possible 'so what?' when you get there, especially if you're very busy and you've turned it into an 'I must go and see. . .' occasion. In the early part of the year, when the weather can be a bit forbidding, much better to have what you can indoors to brighten your life.

The other thing I do with tulips (but it's probably illegal now) is when they stop flowering I put them on the compost heap. They sometimes flower again there and that's an unusual and brightening sight when you have to take the peelings out. It is still possible as I write to obtain tulips quite inexpensively from wholesale bulb sellers who are willing to sell in some quantity to private individuals, like Peter Nyssen. And then you can try some other colours and colour combinations next year, and you don't need to do all that storing them and protecting them from mice and rot and mildew: someone else is kindly doing all that for you. Buy from them, support their worthy activity. And chuck the tulips out after.

I HATE GARDENING

I hate gardening. I have four acres of garden to make and care for practically single handed, and the work involved is – work.

I recently sat in a hall full of worthy garden professionals and RHS members who were debating 'Is gardening still core to the British way of life?' Speaker after speaker got up and extolled the virtues and delights of gardening. I felt as if I was on a foreign planet. Outside it has been pouring with rain for weeks. Everything is sodden and disintegrating, and I need to get out there because there are things that need to be done. It will be cold, wet and horrible and so shall I be by the time I come in. Can anyone seriously enjoy planting bulbs? I wasn't made with a hinge in my back and my left hip is beginning to protest loudly at the pressure exerted by plunging the bulb planter.

A quarter of garden work is probably planting things; a half of it is cutting things down, cutting them back and pulling them out. This is relentless: I no sooner cut things down than they're up again. It's as bad as weeding, which at least as a glyphosate user I can do standing up. How on earth can the organic lot, condemned to their knees in a truly endless task of pulling things out, enjoy gardening? Are they deluded? Don't they notice? Are they endlessly worshipping their weeds?

Gardening is talked-up housework that you have to do outside. It has everything in common with housework, even some of the tools. I have a vacuum cleaner that I use indoors and out since it sucks up wet as happily as dry. Gardening has a great deal of the same objectives as housework and is mostly depressingly judged on the same kind of criteria – is it neatandtidy and is it weed-free, alongside is it neatandtidy and is it dust-free? It has the same sort of status except among the seriously sad.

Gardening is boring. It is repetitious, repetitive and mind-blowingly boring, just like housework. All of it – sowing seeds, mowing, cutting hedges, potting up, propagating is boring, and all of it requires doing over and over again. If there are enjoyable jobs they're mostly enjoyable for the result not the process.

There is no actual intellectual content to the task itself, even if there may be in the planning and designing. So, if there is something wrong in my world, if an editor has snubbed me or a call centre driven me round the bend, I find myself obsessing. I think we are supposed to be delighting in being out in the open air, communing with nature, but me, I'll be obsessing, writing rude letters in my head. Wishing I was sitting comfortably indoors writing rude letters.

There was even talk in this RHS debate about the great virtues of double digging. Double digging is not only bad for your back (and boring): it is totally unnecessary. It's a kind of horticultural joke and does more harm to the soil than good. Why are we promoting masochism?

The RHS have also been terribly keen on getting children interested in gardening, and indeed this is a preoccupation among many gardeners and garden professionals. I have absolutely no idea why. It's a hopeless career for all but the totally dedicated. And as a hobby? Whoever pursues that which was shoved at them in youth? And why does it matter whether they do or don't? I asked on Twitter and got a variety of answers: to make them love the earth, it's good exercise, so parents can have help weeding and can spend time outside without the children complaining (Excuse me! Why would the children care where their parents are as long as they're off their backs?), to teach patience and many other, unspecified, lessons. But I have a wide range of followers on Twitter, including artists, foodies, interior designers, historians, politicians, and what was striking was that while the gardeners on Twitter broke out into a hot clamour of tweets about all the different reasons why, not one non-gardener thought it mattered at all. And I still, despite all the clamour, don't understand why there is such evangelical zeal. What other pursuit, however worthy, is inflicted on children in this way? Plenty of time to discover the delights and horrors of gardens when you're grown up.

There are enemies out there in the garden too. Not just the neighbours who have to restrain themselves from throwing bricks at our garden visitors because they find them so irritating. No – the 'wildlife'. In this part of the world we have rabbits, deer, wild boar, squirrels, panthers, rats – you name something that the British Isles foster and which is damaging to gardens and we have them. Just down the road in the Forest of Dean they have rambling sheep wandering the roads and gardens; some people get visitations from cows, and this doesn't do the vegetation much good at all.

And a shadow hangs over all, always: how will I cope with all this gardening in ten years' or twenty years time? What kind of nightmare have I created for myself because I cannot contemplate leaving this place? I find it hard enough to go away for the night. And should I care that it will all change irrevocably after I'm gone, when it might well get gardened by idiots or built over? I know I'm not supposed to mind, but I do.

I realize that at this point I'm supposed, by the rules of rhetoric, to relent and acknowledge in a gently humorous way that I am really one of the gang, and I do really like getting out there and dirty. Well, it's sometimes not as bad as I think it will be. Mostly it offers a sense of relief from the oppression of knowing a job needs doing and is sitting there waiting for me. Usually, job done, I come in with a sense of relief, and that is a pleasure. And a sense of exhaustion, which can be another kind of pleasure. The best bit is the hot bath.

What I do like is a garden and I have no other means of obtaining one. In a gardening world obsessed with plants and with the delights of gardening, this puts me in a very small minority. But for me the point is the product.

Not a showplace for plants. Not an outdoor gym. Not even a nature reserve. A garden, designed and planted to give delight to the eye and the realization of a fantasy about what could possibly be made with the shape of the land, with plants, with the work of the seasons and the weather. This is the point of it all and it is worth all the rest – just. I think. Maybe. Yes.

THINGS I DON'T DO
Turn my compost heap.
Wash my pots.
Clean my garden tools.
Edge the grass.
Grow veg. (Yes, well . . .)
Dig up plants and divide them.
Put out slug traps.
Spike, weedkill, aerate, topdress,
 remove moss from, worm-kill,
 water, roll or lime the lawn.
Graft.
Dig.
Lime.

Clean the greenhouse (!).
Remove leaves from borders.
Remove anything from borders.
 Let it rot where it grew.
Label plants.
Mulch at some particular time
 of year.

THINGS I DON'T OFTEN DO
Feed plants in borders.
Sharpen my tools.
Deadhead.
Prune.
Stake (except vampires).

OBJECTS

It is generally assumed that a garden needs objects – statues, sculptures, pots, fountains and so on – to create focal points and contrasts to the flowery or planty material in the garden. It doesn't need to be the case – what might be in a garden or not is up to the gardener. I needed objects: not everyone will.

Objects are problematic, though. The best tend to be expensive. A specially commissioned sculpture, anyone? That would enable you to decide just what the sculpture would be about, its size and form and style, but basically and unfortunately (for who would not wish to support and encourage an artist or craftsman?) most of us would need to win the lottery to think of it. And even to buy a pre-existing piece is not going to be affordable for me.

Times change and what goes around, they say, comes around. I've never quite understood that expression, but I get the message and I've seen it in gardening. Just as 'grow your own' is now coming around for the second (or third?) time in my garden career, so is recycling. It used to be seen simply in terms of reuse of that which could be found in junk yards and reclamation yards. Bits of old machinery, bashed-about, rusting metal seats, the washing copper which became and has probably stayed totally desirable and so totally unaffordable, but which typifies the type of object considered covetable. Unfortunately, anything of any size – and even in a small space you need as big as possible, or it'll look twee – is still expensive. This used to apply indoors too, before Ikea. We all used to get old furniture, sometimes off skips, and strip and repaint and generally customize. It was fun and terribly tedious and labour-intensive, but we are still using a skip rescue in our sitting room.

We relied on that stuff when we first came here, and even found a small statue in an antique shop in Brighton which we brought proudly home for all its rather sentimental aspect. We needed such a thing as a focal point to the end of the path down the meadow, and this came from an *antique* shop. Afterwards we began to see it everywhere and we realized with great embarrassment that it was a modern manufacture of very dubious taste. We instantly went off it and quietly gave it away to a friend with absolutely no taste at all, instead of a little bit. (Though I know it gave me real pleasure, catching sight of it at the end of the path through the arch, before disillusionment day. Interesting.)

The problem with junk was not just that it was junk, but that it said nothing about who we are, what we intended or thought about the garden or wished the garden to communicate – it was just meaningless decoration. I realized that my ability to make enamels and possession of the relevant equipment opened up possibilities and for a time we added enamel figures, created out of marine ply and loads of small pieces of enamelled copper. Gaudy (Gaudi?) but possible. Eventually we went off that as well – the major piece I did never looked quite right and in the end we suddenly found it unbearable. Too shiny, perhaps. But there is still a lizard rotting slowly in a tree in the wood.

And in the wood we also added a television, in a spirit of sudden fun. The Welsh tend to abandon their machinery in the fields, and indeed, not a hundred yards from the television in the wood is an ancient car in a neighbour's field – it was ancient when we came here over twenty years ago. Seemed right to join in. Visitors who venture into the woods seem to enjoy the joke. I hope that the plastic television and seat point up, by contrast, the beauty of the wood, which otherwise in a densely wooded county like Monmouthshire could well go unremarked.

BELOW LEFT A homemade lizard of enamels and plywood, slowly rotting up a tree.
BELOW RIGHT For visitors who get bored . . .

The best of the television in the wood was when *Dragon's Eye*, the Welsh *Newsnight*, filmed here, using metaphor from the garden to comment on the scandal of MPs' expenses. In their film they had the presenter sitting on the plastic chair, commenting on Prime Minister's questions, which was showing, live, on the television in the wood.

The risk with using junk, though, apart from junk rage, is that it can add to that woeful weakness of the British garden, visual fuss. It's rare for junk to come with the strong, clean lines which we need in our objects to offset the pervasive bittiness of foliage and flower of the majority of our garden plants. The search for a strong, clean leaf takes us mostly only to hostas, which we then arrange to have shredded by snails, to return them to the familiar and maybe comfortable bittiness. When people do start finding strong contrasting leaves, strangely they don't then use them judiciously to enhance the usual herbaceous planting. They go mad and make one of those 'tropical gardens' which are supposed to amaze us all but which, perhaps inevitably, look terribly samey and, ummm, maybe a bit tropical. But then the ubiquitous bitty garden is even more

BELOW A homemade cut-out buzzard in the crescent border. It glows eerily after sunset.
OPPOSITE Another homemade cut-out, in the vegetable plot, surrounded by aconitums and seedheads of *Clematis orientalis*.

repetitious, so one shouldn't complain.

And the junk collection also can grab hold of people in the same, mad, 'must collect these' mood. A rare, well-designed garden got a fit of this 'litter with rust' mania, and together with an attitude about paths (they positively liked them weedy) killed the contrast of straight clean lines with great planting which had previously made the garden so worth the trip.

So it's a shame really that I have seen the odd, ominous signs of a return to junk gardens, lauded in the name of 'recycling'. Not a happy prospect. The smug, self-righteous 'grow your own' return is bad enough – though that will possibly vanish faster than rusty rubbish, under the weight of relentless work, weeds, creeping creatures and embarrassing gluts.

But the problem remains, what do we use for 'objects'? In the end I took up cut-outs (cut out of plywood). They offered free expression, which meant I could continue to address my homage to the locality, they are simple to produce and they are relatively inexpensive. Not universally liked, but what, in our garden, is?

THE VEG PLOT

We used to have a potager. There was a time when such things were absolutely the thing to have, as compulsory as being green, sustainable or xeriscaping today. Rosemary Verey had one, admired by multitudes, though multitudes could not get to see it because it was designed for one mincing human being to negotiate delicately and sideways. The paths were tiny. This did not stop the adulation – of that and the laburnum tunnel with alliums which appeared relentlessly on every magazine cover, or failing that, several times inside the covers.

We fell in love with the look – and that was a style made to suit Charles's precise and painstaking approach. So he made us one. We couldn't bring ourselves to call it a 'potager', though. It became the veg plot, and despite total lack of edible veggies now it still retains the name. He had enormous fun with coloured lettuces, purple cabbages and who knows what else, all grown in beautiful patterns. We had a farmer visit once – I thought he was going to have a heart attack he was so offended by the sight. It is quite amazing just how powerfully aspects of gardens can upset people, considering what a safe and cosy occupation it's supposed to be.

The veg plot when it was the veg plot. Too much work for boring old veggies. *Rosa* 'Iceberg' as standards – always a risk in gales and far too white in this context, nasturtiums, kale 'Cavolo Nero' and 'Red Bor' with box balls and cabbages in September. Did look good.

People used to fret a lot then that removing a lettuce from a pattern would destroy the pattern and I discovered it didn't. The eye fills in the missing parts for a long time. It is perhaps a little like our ability with music to hear just a little of a melody to know where it will go next. And as with music we probably delight equally in having a pattern fulfilled in the way we expect it to or having it take off in some unexpected and novel direction, confounding our expectation. Pattern and melody are special, I believe linked, and both currently underrated.

Part of the pattern was a series of Iceberg roses, grown as standards, one to each bed apart from where we have standard hollies. Every summer we have a gale at some point and every summer we sweated over the standards and whether they would survive. One day a visitor expressed her sympathy for the fact that the standard rose had blown over – and a quick dash down to the veg plot confirmed that she was right. On other occasions it would just be one of the branches blown out. A lot of grief. Then Clive Nichols confronted us with that which we had carefully been avoiding acknowledging: the harsh white of the roses was totally wrong in that space. It is a very difficult colour to accommodate; he was quite right, and they came out. Relief.

So we used to grow a great variety of veggies and salad. One of my (how come it was me?) most dreaded tasks was planting the potatoes. And the results were never so wonderful or as specially delicious as they are talked up to be. The potatoes tasted like potatoes – and not a patch on shop-bought Jersey Royals, whatever variety we grew (and, yes, we grew all the most fashionable ones). Same with all the rest. Just vegetables with more slugs hiding in them than commercially grown ones.

And they needed picking and preparing . . . In summer you can garden till very late in the evening. So there I'd be, garden, garden, garden, and then suddenly realize supper had to be made. And that that involved all that picking and preparing before I could get anywhere near the cooking. Runner beans were the exception – and I may persuade Charles to grow those again. Better than the shop ones because they will be crisp. Not inclined to slug infestation. Easy to grow, pick and prepare. As long as you cut them on the slant so they stay nice big, crisp pieces. Please don't try and pretend they are those wangy French beans and cut them deviously into strips. I will not be fooled or pleased.

Charles began to take garden photographs professionally and with that and pensionable work was far too busy to go on with the tedious, detailed work that growing veggies in patterns is. Part of the original need – the lack of variety or range in the local shops – had gone. Fruit and vegetables that had been unobtainable were suddenly with us in abundance. We decided to abandon the vegetables and salads, which left a large area to replant – and how?

It was great planning something new effectively from scratch. I have always loved the sculptural leaves of cardoons, and they would, as it were, curtsy to the history of the plot, so we obtained, mostly by seed, ornamental cardoons (*Cynara cardunculus* 'Florist Cardy'), enough to fill the plot. Then to complement and edge them, lots of *Heuchera villosa* 'Palace Purple', because they come easily from seed too, as well as being a great colour to go with the steely grey of the cardoons. It works as well as things ever do in a garden – cardoons look good from spring until July, a good five months. Instead of being grateful we lament how they come up to flower, look magnificent and then topple over in a summer gale or go manky. We are never quite sure if clever management would prevent some of that: I have tried cutting them down as they approach flowering and think they then revive well, but does that weaken the plant in the long term? And anyway, Charles won't part with the flowers, in spite of the fact that falling over, they could clobber someone with all the force and effect of a mace.

We continued for a while to grow fruit under an ugly fruit cage, which led to stand-offs every winter as Charles asserted that it wouldn't snow so we didn't need to remove the netting roof. It was a nasty job, so I would go along with that absurd prediction and then find myself taking it off single-handed in the inevitable blizzard. Eventually I went on strike and the whole thing was spectacularly destroyed by a very heavy snowstorm. We still miss the raspberries especially but we would have a buy a great many punnets of them over many years to make it economical to replace the fruit cage. And when we buy them instead of grow them we don't have to fight off the squirrels, which made holes in the cage, which Charles repaired with fishing line, which then got broken into bigger holes which birds got in through and had to be rescued/chased out.

And the fruit cage was ugly. So, here was an opportunity to replace ugly with – what? The fruit cage area was right next to the veg plot, so they needed to harmonize. So we planted up the area with a mix of purple (brown) shrubs and silver (grey) shrubs. I am really looking forward to seeing the cardoons and heuchera with a backcloth of echoing colours – but there's many a catastrophe between dream and realization in the garden . . .

The veg plot as it is now, under its new name of 'Charles's garden'. Box balls, *Cynara cardunculus* 'Florist Cardy', *Heuchera* 'Palace Purple', *Allium* 'Purple Sensation'. Simpler, easier and probably even better looking.

THE TOUR

It was particularly slow this week when we opened the garden. It is a bit miserable sitting there on the first fine Sunday for several weeks and no one coming. Then a few did – and they were returners. Which did cheer me up, especially since one family had been last week and were returning because it was their last chance before going back home from their holiday; *and* they claimed not to be gardeners.

And then a regular, annual returner, who tells me she comes regularly because it is so special and because it is so peaceful after a hard week. We got into discussion about gardens and at some point she told me she had brought some friends here once – 'but they didn't understand it.'

Now this isn't the first time the issue of understanding the garden has arisen, though I have not followed it up before. This time I asked for an explanation and it was to do with not being able to see the 'whole' but wondering why there was so much willowherb – rueful smile.

I know people come to look at plants, and I know they would come in greater numbers to buy them if I offered. And if we did teas I could start counting the garden a real success . . . But not understanding is slightly different. After all, it's not a Conceptual Garden in the orange plastic sense. We have flowers, lots of them, and I would have thought a not totally unfamiliar layout – 'garden rooms', mixed borders, that kind of thing. A meadow . . . Now there's a thing. There was a time when people actually didn't understand that: years ago I was asked if I intended to keep some geese by someone looking for an explanation of the phenomenon of a meadow in a garden. Now, in the right season, people enthuse about it greatly – as they should because it is truly beautiful. But for the general public to have arrived in a place where they can appreciate that beauty it seems a change of perception had to take place, a new idea had to enter the garden lexicon. Which suggests that a garden *does* have to be understood: that when we enter a garden we enter it full of preconceptions which then dictate how and what we see.

In the same conversation with my garden visitor I asked her what she thought about doing guided tours. I have always felt uncomfortable about doing these, but have responded when asked to. Maybe because I'm boring or I haven't got the right knack, I have usually found that halfway through people are drifting off.

That has never disturbed me because I think the best way to enjoy a garden is to wander at will without the proud owner wittering in your ear.

I also believe that if you assume that everything about a work of art is considered and purposeful you must then begin to examine your own responses if you find something odd, jarring or different about it. So, adopting such an approach, a visitor here might, all of their own accord, see willowherb or ground elder and begin to work out for themselves what it is offering. They might question their own assumptions about maintenance style and consider what is appropriate in a country setting. They might consider the particular contribution these plants are making. They might examine the headstones in the wild garden and work out that they are place names and that the numbers look a great deal like dates and . . . Or they might just read the free leaflet about it which they have in their hand. But their best starting point would surely be to assume that everything that is in the garden is meant to be the way it is.

However, I began to question that delightful fantasy when I visited a National Trust house and found that when the enthusiastic room volunteers told us about the rooms we were in, I was suddenly seeing things I hadn't noticed, or seeing them with greater interest because of the background information I was offered. Hence my asking our visitor what she thought. And she thought similarly, that you see 'differently' when someone explains – and she gave as an example how reading about the Veddw, though she is very familiar with it, had changed some of her perceptions of it, enriching her experience of it.

Thinking about all this I remembered my days as a total garden novice. I remembered going to Sissinghurst and being totally bewildered. I found the messiness strange. The rose garden had roses which had gone over. Nothing strange about that, except that from my – just beginning to make a garden – perspective, it seemed strange. I had been puzzling about how to avoid such a hiatus (I still do) yet here, in this major garden, the roses were just there, offering nothing and looking, frankly, a bit of a mess.

At the time it gave me permission to be a little less demanding, but I believe I hear something of the same confusion now from my visitors. Many of them no doubt have smaller gardens and keep them quite differently, so they would find my maintenance style bewildering, and this may be seen as an issue of tidiness. But more than that: I am after a different result. Not specifically *untidiness*, but a more natural, informal style than perhaps they are used to or expect.

And the willowherb: I am looking for effect, even from those plants which people may regard as weeds and can only see as weeds. I have an area which I am waiting for a rambler rose to cover, as ground cover, so I have encouraged ground elder to spread. It has a good leaf, does the covering job enthusiastically, keeps the

The beauty of ground elder. (Call it *Aegopodium podagraria* and it becomes respectable. Maybe.)

ground clean of other, unwanted plants, is easy to maintain with a strim at flowering time (the flowers make it just look weedy) and provides a good floor for the rose to cover in its turn (the perfect garden plant, really).

A.C. Grayling says rightly, in *The Mystery of Things*, that 'one more richly appreciates an author's work after learning about the circumstances of its creation and about the author's character and life.' So perhaps people need help to see the point of ground elder and willowherb and the virtues of a relaxed country style. Not just to see beyond ground elder and willowherb being weeds, but also to see the virtues I find in a mass of low-growing, classy-leaved plant as opposed to, or in contrast with, a multicoloured, multi-planted border of mixed perennials or bedding plants. Maybe they need to be introduced to the idea of a garden needing a quiet passage occasionally, so that all is not restless busyness. And the idea of introducing words and ideas into a garden may well be new and strange for some.

This may be a question with no right answers. There will be a freshness to visiting a garden without information or preconceptions, and a depth to visiting it with knowledge and understanding. The ideal has got to be to do both, perhaps in a different season to add even more to your understanding.

SNOWDROPS
AND AMBIVALENCE

OK, I may hate gardening, but the slightest glow of winter sunshine draws me irresistibly outside. The sun is lost to this garden for a few weeks in the winter, because we are sheltered by a high ridge to the south. (The apparent contradiction of being sheltered from the warm side rather than the more challenging north arises because the ridge extends far enough to also deflect the prevailing wind from the south-west.) When the sun returns to the garden it can feel as if the spring has sprung and whereas for eleven months of the year I wilt with boredom at the idea of snowdrops, come January I'm off out looking for them.

I think it's basically an excuse to be outside. I pick some, and then I glance approvingly at them in a vase for a few days. Then I scowl at them for a few days as they go brown, until at last, in an uncharacteristically housewifely frame of mind, I throw them out. I follow a similar routine with sarcococca, but this has the added advantage of being the best pluckable scent in the garden, one which really does do that fabled and elusive thing, 'scent a room'.

I do not crawl about on my hands and knees in the winter mud gawping at endless variations on the form of the snowdrop flower. Or variations on the length of its stalk or a touch of yellow where the green should be. I have never understood this obsession, but then I don't dwell much on the subtle beauty of any flower. I like to mass them, use them, sculpt with them; make pictures in the landscape which capture the imagination. I think there are probably two kinds of lookers, besides the supermodel kind. Those who have patience and appetite for detail and those like me who love the broader effect. I'm the same with books: I want to understand what someone is saying, dive in for the meaning rather than dwell on the beauty of the expression. I rush along, impatient with self-conscious language that merely demands that I notice and admire it. The same with plants.

Those like me are overpowered by the rest. The garden world is full of the relentless plant detail which fills the yawning garden pages. At this time of year it is in relatively short supply, so that having had magazines and newspapers full of holly and ideas for tree planting, we will now have the annual trawl through snowdrops and hellebores and winter aconites followed by those cute little daffodils, *so* much better than their coarse overblown relatives featuring on roundabouts. (This was written just before an apparent resurgence in interest in the wonderful history and products of hybridization in the narcissi – are big daffs back?)

The need for endless soothing and repetitive articles conjuring up a never-never land of spotless plants inevitably sidelines people like me. I have come to hate the idea of being 'passionate about my garden, passionate about plants'. The result is that I keep my vice to myself, so much so that I even deceive myself in December and begin to believe that I could shed the garden and all its work and works and take to a library to indulge the study of history. Come January and the sun I'm off out there again. What for? I hardly know. A compulsion to see what's happening? To have another look, to kick over a molehill and see if I can discover where the b— rabbit is coming from?

In other words, I am deeply ambivalent about that lot outside. I do feel glad to see the isolated but still reappearing snowdrops of some particular and special kind reappearing. I got them when I interviewed a snowdrop fan for an article on her tiny winter-flowering garden. I fell for the idea of a few specials, and here I am, welcoming them back again, even though they're hardly thriving and spreading. Why? I feel a little flattered maybe, that they haven't totally shunned me. Intrigued to see what's special about them, because I really have no idea, can't remember a thing about them, especially their names. I was recently reproached by a garden club I spoke to for my failure to remember the names of the (very ordinary) plants in my own garden. It seems sympathy for the disabled has not spread to garden-club land, or the members there are still blissfully unaware of the crippling effects of middle age on the names bit of our brains.

I won't be doing anything with these snowdrops. They are only just hanging on; I can't upset them by picking any stems for the rotting-in-the-house routine. I will watch them come out, examine them at least once and leave them be. And greet them in this desultory manner every year that they deign to reappear. Mutual tolerance. If they don't ask anything of me, I won't ask anything of them. OK.

THE REFLECTING POOL

ITS ORIGINS

My experience of leaning over the wall of the terrace pool enjoying the reflections in the evening led me to want to do this properly, where there wouldn't be a reflection of a (now blessedly disappeared) telegraph pole. The obvious place for a reflecting pool was in one of the empty yew gardens. The hedges had now created the enclosures and the enclosures were waiting for gardens. Blissful and agonizing deciding how to deploy them.

This particular space was fairly flat. At least, it looked fairly flat to me. In the event it turned out to have a drop on the diagonal of four feet, so some hefty filling and retaining had to be done. Besides being flattish, this area looked into a garden beyond it – and then beyond that again was the coppice: the reflection to be, I sort of hoped. I really had no idea exactly what would reflect into it, never having been able to quite get comfortable with the physics of reflections, though I was fairly confident the sky would feature. I tried a mirror but it was hardly illuminating.

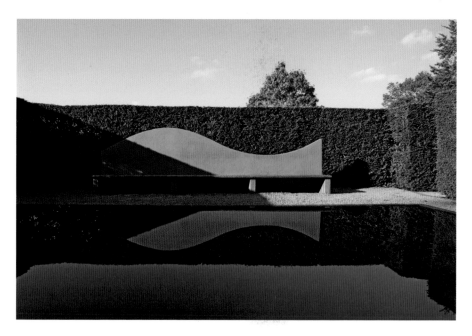

The in-between garden was clearly not flat. It would be an important view from my dream pool. This garden had an even bigger diagonal slope – what to do? Pictures of Piet Oudolf's garden told me: shaped hedges. We alternated their open ends so that walking through them became a bit like travelling an unproblematic maze and the slope became an advantage, because the hedges could read against each other all the way up that garden. This began to be very exciting but meanwhile we had years of sitting shouting shaping instructions to each other in our attempt to make the hedges the right shapes to read well. Hardest when they were tiny and the plants hardly met each other sideways.

The result is that the curves of the first hedges reflect into the water, with the trees beyond, which look especially wonderful with sunlight through them or on them. Then above the view of the reflection in the pool we see the pattern of the hedges, formal and satisfying, backed by the mature beeches and oak behind the coppice.

Before all this could happen, though, we needed the pool. I measured and discovered that I could use the magic proportions of the Golden Rectangle.

OPPOSITE A homemade bench. I designed it low and wide for comfort, big to fill the space. It was coloured and shaped for drama and to echo the hedges and soil of the landscape.
BELOW A view across the reflecting pool to the hedge garden, with the coppice behind. The hedge garden is still working up to size at the back, so it's still fuzzy.

Anyone who is designing a structure such as a formal pool in the garden needs to know the Golden Rectangle, even if they don't understand it, because it miraculously produces a harmonious and pleasing shape. I don't think anyone really knows why human beings find it so satisfying, but it seems that the Fibonacci series is the basis for much of nature's geometry, and the Golden Rectangle is based on the Fibonacci series (please don't ask me how). The proportions for the Golden Rectangle are 21/34 – so if you were to make your pool 21 feet × 34 feet (or 10.5 feet × 17 feet) you are very likely to like the result and please your guests. (Even if they aren't looking at it from above? Well, maybe I'm imagining that the pleasingness belongs to Fibonacci.) Anyway, that was what I based my plan on.

Then having decided absolutely that I must have this pool I immediately ran into the obvious problem: cost. Our first quote was for over £10,000 plus VAT and therefore unimaginable. Back to the drawing board . . . Stuck.

I then remembered having seen something about a pool which was two inches deep – a large bird bath in effect. I still think that an enormous bird bath is a sweet idea, but I went slightly deeper – six inches. (It would drown most birds, sadly.) This was transforming, because it solved all sorts of problems.

It is much cheaper to have a shallow pool. The engineering is less dramatic because the weight of water is so much less (water being very heavy). And there is less spoil to be removed – in our case it just got shuffled about the site to help adjust those terrible levels. And then it's easier to care for – it gets cleaned every year by emptying because there is relatively little water there to either drain or replace.

So I got my reflecting pool and it was and is everything I dreamt of.

THE EXPERIENCE OF THE POOL

Contemplating writing about the reflecting pool confronts me perhaps most of all with the problem of what really matters to me in the garden and the banality of saying anything about it. Obviously, if I could have said what I want to say in writing I wouldn't have done it on the ground. Perhaps the garden speaks for itself? But if I am to write about it I have to try to convey something of what it means to me and why, or all I have is 'how to and where to' and that is a travesty of what the garden is about. It is not a horticultural exercise or a collection of plants.

The idea, the meaning, the importance of the reflecting pool for me is in the continual experience of it.

But often and perhaps regrettably that experience produces not peaceful reflection but a rush for the camera. Sometimes the sun will shine through the trees beyond the hedge garden and the beauty of that light and its reflection will induce silent, reverent contemplation. For all of a couple of minutes . . . before I feel compelled to try and capture that wonderful sight, even though I'm not photographer.

Sometimes the pool is full of debris, leaves or hedge clippings, even algae, and my experience then is of having to clean it before I, or anyone else, can enjoy it. But this is always true of the garden – the experience of it changes depending on how I approach it and what state and season it is in.

Putting all that aside, the reflecting pool is powerful. It holds memories and moments: the past and the present. And in this it concentrates within it the nature of the whole garden.

We spent one evening photographing as night came on, with nightlights all around the pool edge and the giant hogweed in the distance spotlit. We've made love there. Ritually eaten ice cream there. Discussed divorce there – and then, with horror, recognized the power that we both have in relation to each other: the power to take the garden away and banish us both like Adam and Eve.

We've sat there with wine and

The reflecting pool doing what it does best. Beech, oak and *Magnolia stellata* behind and reflected.

many friends, visitors, television crews. We've entertained people's fantasies there – Charles's favourite, of a kind of Captain Pugwash scene, with a boat sailing up and down on the hedges. This leads to other people's fantasy puppet shows – one which was to take place in the trees on a high wire with a lady trapeze artiste doing her Edwardian stuff. The fantasy depths of the pool have produced other worlds of mystery and presumably wetness. The Pool Garden seems to stimulate fantastic trips of imagination. And laughter – a recurring fantasy has been an arm rising out of the water, 'Clothed in white samite, mystic, wonderful', offering Excalibur. But the pool is only six inches deep, so someone suggested a *miniature* arm . . .

I sat there with Piet Oudolf and was able to thank him for the inspiration of the hedges. And he told me how he had seen a picture of the pool and said to himself that he would never actually see that place – but then, unexpectedly and surprisingly, here he was.

We redraw the hedges, endlessly, with hedge cutters. Visitors theoretically and sometimes troublingly suggest different patterns: disturb the symmetry of the first pair by letting one grow a buttress? Disturb perfection?

I contemplate the future and think it may be a relief to move one day. To shed the work, the aggravation, the fears, expense, headaches. But then someone else would believe this pool to be theirs. As long as I am alive to know it, that feels totally outrageous. And what about the others who would then also be excluded? Good friends whose friendships with me were created out of this garden and who in their encouragement helped create it? Sara Maitland, who came to research her book *Gardens of Illusion* and stayed in my life, was the first person who actually understood what I was doing and she then iced that cake by writing about it – giving me hope that one day others would follow with equal sensitivity. The idea that the gate would close against her and the other friends the garden has brought is unthinkable, terrible and, of course, true.

I know people talk a lot of pious nonsense about gardens – that they don't stand still, that they should be permitted to change after the creator's death, that they as creator think that is all jolly good and OK. It is not. It is horrendous. This is me and it is us and it – and we – should be here, just this way, forever. Everyone knows that; why pretend otherwise? And it is the garden all the time that reminds us of our mortality, as a garden is totally reflective of time and in a garden time is inescapable. Death is here. And it is not welcome. I will not pretend I have come to terms with death or my fate, Charles's fate or the fate of the garden. I can wake in a cold sweat terrified by the knowledge that all this and us will inevitably end, and I live with that knowledge only by ignoring it most of the time. Though sometimes I also stare it in the face in the hope that I can learn to bear it.

ALCHEMILLA MOLLIS

I have met gardeners who make the sign of the cross at the sight of alchemilla. This is because it seeds itself so generously. Well, be grateful that there is such a beautiful, essential plant that does that for us and then find a good use for it.

I use it to spare me that dreadful sight of grass and border kept apart by an edging tool. There are one or two truly awful things to do to a garden. Among them is using an edging tool to create a rigid separation between plants and soil. It's ugly, unnecessary and a work creator. How many hours do people mindlessly

A ribbon of *Alchemilla mollis* runs alongside the lawn, opposite the crescent border with *Campanula lactiflora* and *Chamerion angustifolium* 'Stahl Rose'. We fortunately got rid of the phormium, which started off looking good and ended up – well, as you see.

spend chopping carefully away at their turf when they could be reading a good book? There are various answers to the problem and one of the best is alchemilla. (Other ones are making a mowing line of concrete or stone paving along the edge, strimming the edge carefully or having a low, containing hedge and strimming up to it.)

I love the ribbon of alchemilla that runs along the edge of the lawn with a graceful curve at either end, like an elongated 's'. From the time it emerges in the spring to its death in early winter it is a satisfying sight. Everyone knows, but it bears reminding, that rain stays sparkling in the crinkled leaves for long after the shower is over. Not everyone knows that if you grow it along your lawn edge you can mow it off after the flowers go over, reducing the seedlings if you don't want them. (Though watch where you put your mowings! Unless, of course, you want an easy way to sow lots of alchemilla.) And then it reappears, fresh and new, within a week.

Many men dislike the flowers of alchemilla. I suspect because they don't have the form and colour of conventional flowers and many men are deeply conventional in the garden. Whereas many women get obsessed with plant collecting and will forgive a plant almost anything for being different. Me, I just think it's the icing on the cake, and I love icing.

STATUS

This could be a very difficult topic: I'm sure that to a person preoccupied by trees or compost making there are special heroes and villains. But I'm prepared to generalize here and speak just from the perspective of someone whose garden world is informed by opening a garden, writing about gardens and having a photographer for a husband. And I'm not talking about my own private status hierarchy, but that which I perceive around me.

Depressing as it is, I suspect that TV celebrities come top. Someone has stuck their neck out recently with a blog which is prepared to be mildly critical of some aspects of the garden world. But praise for the ubiquitous Carol Klein pops in. Why her? There is a kind of adulation of the well known in the blogosphere. So with all the TV celebs. And they are inescapable – they even impinge on someone like myself who rarely watches any of them: their names pop up all over the place to sell us things. The BBC maintains two magazines to promote them.

Their status declares itself rather graphically at Chelsea Press Day. Periodically all the also-rans are herded out of the way as the BBC cameras heave into sight, take over all available space and some television personality does their stuff, while the rest of us stand and watch, gossiping in a deprecatory and comforting way. The BBC puts large funds into the show and so is absolutely entitled to take over bits of it for large chunks of time, but the manner of the exercise puts the rest of us solidly in our place. The TV celebs also seem curiously disconnected because they have mega status but must needs cater to the lowest common denominator, so I'm not sure they command general respect with other garden professionals, unless they have an encyclopaedic knowledge of plants. (That, in the garden world, inevitably confers godlike stature.)

The other, rather more upmarket mega stars also appear at Chelsea: the star designers. They do seem to command respect, to the extent that they are liberated from the requirement of being walking plant encyclopaedias. But, of course, they are also on trial at Chelsea: does their latest effort hit the spot? And on Press Day they have to 'chat' to whoever successfully collars them, which is not very status-full. But we all know they have it in varying degrees: and interestingly the ones contaminated by their television appearances again come bottom of this particular subsection of the status list. Not taken terribly seriously, especially the ones inclined to produce pastiche gardens full of flowery nostalgia. Don't know if anyone quite knows where to place Diarmuid these days. Bit of an anomaly, having blown open the cosy television world with a blaze of stunning and innovative gardens, and then somehow been sucked dry by the same ravening TV world. No celebrity is allowed out of the TV world until every last drop has been extracted. If they're lucky they become a national treasure fast and thereby escape the otherwise inevitable 'weary old fart' factor.

Next in the status line appear people associated with gardens, and these are in one of two categories: they were either famous for something else first or they've written about their garden. The first group includes Ian Hamilton-Finlay, Derek Jarman and Charles Jencks (why does Maggie Keswick so rarely receive the appropriate acknowledgement in relation to Portrack?). In fact they *are* the first group. (And two of them are dead.) The second group are all supposedly revered for their gardens, but in fact in every case it has been *writing* about their gardens which has bestowed the status. (And now I'm at it too – so you may guess why.) This group includes Penelope Hobhouse, Beth Chatto and, across the water, Helen Dillon. (Rosemary Verey and Christopher Lloyd belonged here too.) And various 'almost but not quites': probably having failed by being not quite serious or weighty enough about their gardens, perhaps.

Some have written and still failed to become starry at all. Others have written and are assumed to have (mysteriously absent) gardens. It really doesn't matter whether they have a garden of note or no garden: if they write *as if* they have one they are credited with one and this adds status. Sometimes people can visit and presumably see there is no garden, but 'Emperor's new clothes' like, they still 'see' one and revere it.

There are many writers, few making a living out of it. They trail along behind the photographers, often visiting a garden out of season or at a different season from the photographer – it seems to be generally agreed that readers don't read: they look at pictures. Writers have nearly as little status as garden owners.

Editors are among the next – rather mixed – bunch. Discounted among many for their credulousness and the fact that they are rooted in a commercial world, into which they may actually vanish, to start editing *Miniature Railways* instead. Their garden perception may be urban and sentimental. Partly because urban is where a lot of publishing takes place.

Most photographers are anonymous to the general public, I believe, apart from a few star names – Andrew Lawson, Jerry Harpur, Clive Nichols, Marianne Majerus. But who else? Photographers' names tend to appear sideways alongside their pictures when published, so presumably they are known to some people who read their papers and magazines sideways.

Nursery men and women slip in somewhere in the starry firmament: better known than photographers, and, in a plant-mad world, bound to acquire people on their coat tails. Glamour attaches to trips abroad known as 'plant collecting' in spite of the fact that some of this collecting is terribly similar to the punters' own plant collecting: that is to say it happens in garden centres and nurseries – just foreign ones in the nurseryman's case.

At the very, very bottom of the heap are garden owners who have not written and who open their gardens to the public. They are regarded with thinly disguised contempt by the 'professionals'. All the 'professionals' feed off them and like all predators they see their prey as rather lower in the food chain than themselves. Gardeners who are flattered into opening their gardens for the National Gardens Scheme expose themselves to this feeding frenzy. Every editor wants new gardens. Their appetite for new gardens is remorseless – and omnivorous. Pictures are what is wanted, pictures of *new* gardens, never-seen-before gardens, lost gardens, forgotten gardens, small gardens, town gardens, communal gardens, roof gardens, secret gardens, any sort of garden just so long as it's *new* (and, preferably, *small* – this is all about the readers being able to imitate, remember).

This keeps photographers busy. As soon as the *Yellow Book* comes out the keenest of them will have their engines running, off after the new gardens. Best if you're in the south-east of England, of course; fewer callers if your garden is in the north of Scotland.

It seems to be generally assumed among garden professionals that garden owners are full of vanity. This idea is reinforced by the willingness with which garden owners expose themselves to loving lenses in the interest of appearing in a magazine. This amounts to free advertising for the garden, which accounts for some of that enthusiasm: numbers are everything in the NGS world.

Some gardens, especially those in public ownership or run by 'trusts', want to charge photographers for the privilege of picture-taking, or ask to acquire special rights over the pictures. They make themselves thoroughly unpopular. But there is no copyright in a garden, only on the photographer's picture, and that is squarely owned by the photographer. It seems irresponsible, to me, that such organizations, when publicly owned or charitable, should shoot themselves in the foot so. They lose valuable publicity by being so demanding, and this costs both the garden and the surrounding tourist attractions.

ARE GARDENS
FOR GARDENERS?

Are people so vulnerable to suggestion that they adjust their critical faculties in accordance with what they are told to admire? Perhaps we are. I found myself struggling with this recently while watching a programme on interior design. We were presented with a 'Venetian palazzo' and shown various rooms with gaudy and uncomfortable pieces of furniture in random colours and styles scattered around enormous rooms, at a scale that would leave the ordinary-sized human being feeling intimidated and overwhelmed. We were required by the presenter to admire it. I struggled a bit: clearly enormous sums of money had been thrown at this project and it was being so talked up. It was intended to impress rather than to welcome or to relax in, so maybe . . . But no. It was awful. I finally allowed myself to acknowledge it.

But note my struggle. I was being 'told', with authority, by an 'expert', that this gilded bling was 'stunning' and it was tempting to believe it. Worse, it was the easy option, the choice that involved no thought and none of the discomfort which comes from striking out and taking a different view. Gullibility is comfortable. This gullibility factor drives the whole engine of the garden media, starting with the editors and their reverence for 'experts'.

Why are we so willing, indeed eager, to be told what to do in our gardens and what to think about them (or, rather, not think about them) by quasi-adult figures, as if we are unusually acquiescent children? It is certain that the garden world as represented by the written media is dominated by an assumption that the reader is a beginner and it is also true that there is a certain amount for a beginner to learn in order to make or maintain a garden. Magazines and the garden sections of newspapers depend on their advertisers, and recently a newspaper editor was kind enough, and frank enough, to spell out the advertisers' preoccupations. They need to perpetuate a readership of the unknowing amateur in order to sell them things. Those of us who have our greenhouses, mowers, seed trays, watering cans and spades are of little interest to the horticultural industry. We can be sold a few peripherals, usually revolting ornaments or, with acknowledgment to our likely age, seats, but we're very marginal. The audience that is wanted are the beginners, the ready market. And in that the infantilizing of gardeners maybe has its origins.

Hence all the 'how to', 'now to' and 'where to' columns which used to so confuse me when I actually was a beginner. I couldn't grasp quite why I was being told how to sow my sweet peas when I had no wish to grow said sweet peas: I hadn't quite got the hang of this ubiquitous advice-giving, which assumes not only we all know nothing but that we're all doing and wishing to do the same things in our gardens.

What is more astonishing, however is how willing people are to go on being treated as ignorant children, asking for advice, being slightly delinquent and both adulating our 'teachers' and wishing to slightly bring them down with a little soft-edged mockery. Blogs are full of this: the 'Garden Monkey', for example, devoted hours and hours to relentless imaginative play involving his or her teachers being in a 'Big Brother House'. Perhaps more amazingly, some minor garden celebs join in, in the same vein. It is clear that many gardeners happily embrace this role, and it may be worth noting that it returns us to a kind of innocent world of childhood where play is all, and thoughtfulness and seriousness have yet to toss us out of Eden.

The willingness of magazine and newspaper editors to proudly show pictures of lots of nothing much at all as long as it's in a garden belonging to a famous garden 'expert' is staggering, but indicates that they know their audience. It's like a sneaky look into teacher's bedroom. The fact that it is worse than unremarkable no doubt passes us by, given its aura of voyeurism. There is more excuse on television for the presentation of the expert's bland and spotty plot because the producer may be less exposed to the garden world and in no position to have developed discrimination, but on the other hand they do get to see more than just pretty pictures of highly selected bits, which is all the editors of the printed media generally get. I suppose neither TV nor newspaper editors take gardens seriously or wish to challenge their audience's lack of sophistication. Why should they?

But the audience's eager wish to suspend their critical faculties extends beyond the gardens of the 'experts' and for some it clearly includes every patch outside anyone's front or back door. Mary Keen reported in the *Telegraph* that when she asked her readers if they wanted truthful reviews of gardens they wrote in great (though unspecified) numbers saying effectively, no, they didn't. She did not seem to find this surprising. (Though when she asked her readers for their favourite gardens the winning garden got seventeen votes, so we may perhaps take this poll with a pinch of scepticism.)

The general impression, of writers, editors, television producers and their audiences is of a kind of *folie à deux*, where everyone endlessly reinforces each other's madness in utter indifference to reality or the outside world. Mary Keen said people thought honest garden reviews would 'tread on their [her readers'] dreams', which fits and reinforces my picture that we are dealing with regression.

I negotiated about writing a book of garden reviews. (Truthful ones.) The publishers couldn't cope with their anxiety that it might *upset* people. This is a common preoccupation of editors of all kinds in the garden world and is one which perhaps is only otherwise applied to small children.

All this preoccupation with fantasy and creating a childlike, innocent world is fed by the dominance in the garden world of the National Gardens Scheme and Scotland's Garden Scheme. These are charitable organizations which raise millions of pounds every year for good causes, as charities are currently called, by inspecting gardens in England and Wales, and Scotland, and then supporting their owners in opening to the public for the NGS charities. These gardens are then advertised in the *Yellow Book*. This organization dominates the garden-visiting scene and the majority of garden visits originate in perusal of the *Yellow Book*. The entries are written by the garden owners, which obviously saves on costs, but equally obviously encourages an uncritical, fantasy view of the gardens.

The innocent playground aspect of gardening is thus exacerbated and a pall of holiness descends over the scene: the gardens may be dreadful, but they open in *a good cause* and anything that is done so worthily must obviously be above and beyond criticism or even the mild exercise of the critical faculties. Lowered voices, hats and a sacred meal (tea!) are involved, and we all know what that means. Free speech is one thing, but some things should not be soiled by it.

However, there are occasionally indications that Satan has his foot in the gate. I have spent time with several garden visitors giggling gleefully about the great pride that various household names take in their dreadful garden efforts or the sad realities of various much-talked-up gardens. Some people – though not nearly enough – get very angry about having been misled. And some people are generally discriminating and critical of the gardens they visit. I discover these things, gossiping with the visitors to our garden on an open day: not all viewers and readers are vulnerable to the fame factor or the authorities telling them what to admire. But these enlightened people are not actually in the majority and I wonder if some of it is any more than the kids' gossip in the playground.

When I appeared on television being critical of gardens, the programmes were seen by over a million people and attracted only one complaint to the production company, and this might appear to suggest that gardeners are more robust than I am indicating. But I suspect these programmes may not have had a typical garden audience. The programmes did not appear on the usual gardens slot on the channel (BBC2) which generally hosts garden programmes and they actually targeted people who had been attached to a programme about houses. And some very angry and abusive comments about me and the process of criticizing gardens did appear in some garden blogs (taking the form, perhaps predictably, of name-calling, school yard style), which may be the only totally free and revealing place for gardeners' expression.

Then there is the question of plants, the holy of holies. It is clear that for most people they are the purpose of a garden, its whole *raison d'être*. The suggestion that gardeners might consider aspects of the design of their gardens can provoke the most amazing howling rage. What is this about?

A dissonance between the process of tending plants and the concept of using them for effect? That begs the question of why on earth there would be such an attitude. There need be no contradiction, you might think, between growing a plant and placing it where it is shown to its best effect. A great deal of lip service is given to growing plants in soil they like, with the degree of sunshine they like and with reference to their hardiness, but the truth is that plants are mostly tough old things that survive a great deal, or alternatively they vanish unless offered great care. You can make a great garden with the former and a – very small – fortune out of the latter. It seems you can write a great deal about both. But you might think there would be no harm in considering if the place suits the plant aesthetically too.

Perhaps the preciousness about plants is informed by a kind of anthropomorphism – that plants are little human beings really and we shouldn't 'use' them, only love them. That would make sense of a lot, but not the fact that people often then proceed to eat them.

However, the unthinking praise that is heaped on gardens is also frequently and equally indiscriminately heaped upon plants. Christopher Lloyd was loved by many gardeners because he was prepared to criticize plants, but he was a rare bird, and I wonder if he would be published in magazines or newspapers today? (Unfortunately he also regarded it as sacrilegious to publically criticize gardens, so his edge only ever extended to plants and occasional goes at gardeners.) He was the exception that proves the rule until Piet Oudolf appeared on the scene. Piet also can be brutally honest about the shortcomings of plants and his books are therefore to be treasured. (Books tend to offer a writer greater freedom of expression than magazines and newspapers.) It is however a hopeful sign, perhaps, that Jane Perrone, editor of the *Guardian* garden pages and website, considers Christopher Lloyd an inspiration.

Is part of the problem the deep conservatism of the garden world, which keeps people locked into a certain set of preoccupations and mindsets? Are there people actually looking forward to the pieces in the magazines about snowdrops in January and whether to cut down their borders in the autumn? Are these a kind of sacred ritual, marking the turning year, a sedentary version of trick or treat?

Why were there never loud protests about the *Telegraph* colour supplement always featuring Lord and Lady so and so and their Labradors in the garden feature? Who knows? Perhaps it is another aspect of the infantilizing process: the *Telegraph* reader having a gawk over the wall at the posh. It is all incredibly depressing, unless you're a garden writer who wishes to write endlessly about snowdrops and whether or not to cut borders down. Or a photographer, longing to take more stunning pictures of hoar frost or lords and ladies (of the human kind).

It could be the nature of gardeners. Most people who possess a garden which could possibly be more than a playground or barbecue site are likely to be middle-aged, given the cost of housing and the ubiquity of small children in the lives of younger people. Could it possibly be that most people's ability to respond positively to new ideas, to be – dreaded word – creative and innovative has passed by this age? Gardens take a long time to mature, meaning that learning can possibly be a slow process too, adding further years to the equation. I decided I didn't want to limit my choices by having children and this gave me the resources to make a garden, however shoestring, while I was quite young. But I am – or was – unusual. This analysis would actually fit well with the idea of gardeners as infantilized, since it is the young who tend to create new worlds, break up traditions and generally go rebellious, and the middle-aged who look back with longing at the school yard.

I yearn for this not to be true, though. And it may be a view rooted in the past. The baby boomers were an innovative, ground-breaking generation – or at least were surrounded by innovation and rule-breaking. Perhaps as we have come to garden-making our special qualities are being ignored in a world full of stereotyping.

If we are to include gardens potentially within the arts we would also have to observe that gardening is usually a self-taught skill, with a little help from the 'experts'. The solitary nature of most garden learning must limit exposure to serious teaching and to other learners – people who might challenge preconceptions and introduce the learner to new ideas and to previous masters of the art.

This leads to another obvious problem: it is possible in gardening to separate the learning of the skills from the expression of the skills. If you learn a musical instrument it is necessary to play something, and it is possible that you will play something good and begin to learn about the music as well as the playing. You learn to act by acting in plays, to dance by dancing in performances, and you used to learn to paint by copying existing exemplars of your art. But you can learn to garden without ever seeing a garden of any merit – indeed, you are likely to do just that. A staggering number of garden owners I came across when writing up gardens for magazines absolutely *prided* themselves on never visiting anyone else's garden. And that is unlikely to inspire you to brilliant composition. Or even, perhaps, to realize that gardens are composed at all. After all, most people proceed with whatever is already outside their house, not a clean slate.

And they have the additional handicap of believing that it is vile and wicked to deliberately kill a plant. (Unless you want to eat it.) So people make their gardens round the existing plants, probably with no thought about the limitations this is unnecessarily imposing, no idea about the possibilities that clearing the site (wicked heresy) to start over would offer. When people were extravagantly throwing away recently installed kitchens in the recent boom years I heard no whisper of gardens also ending up in skips.

Altogether, I have become convinced that if anyone is ever going to appreciate gardens as something more than a plant collection and playground it will not be gardeners. And gardeners will definitely not lead the way to a broader view. This appears counter-intuitive and it has taken me many years to realize it, but it does seem to be the case. And the results of all this are dismal and depressing.

A counter to this is perhaps the attendances at Glastonbury, Glyndebourne and Tate Modern, and the enormous public enthusiasm for the work of artists like Andy Goldsworthy and Antony Gormley. There is a whole world outside the garden ghetto filled with people who are interested in the arts and who could be interested in gardens. There are also still some rich people, who are mercifully not gardeners, who commission exciting gardens.

There are people out there who, I believe, might not be obsessed with collecting plants and may conceive of gardens as more than arrays of interesting or 'unusual' cultivars. There may well be people who have not the slightest wish to plant a poppy or grow a lettuce, but who have an aesthetic sensibility and could understand and enjoy the special power of a place which has been made alongside and in struggle with the natural world, in order to refine or amplify the beauty of nature and the landscape.

We need to reach this world of open-minded, demanding people and patrons – and that is why we have founded thinkingardens (see http://www.thinkingardens). I need to reach them, to preserve my sanity and my belief that the garden I have made is worth refining and improving and suffering for.

It is not going to be easy – it's a bit like trying to climb out of an enormous volcanic crater, and we spend as much time sliding down the sides back into the pit as we do reaching outside it. There is no one on the edge leaning over to lend a hand to pull us out, but there are plenty who are happy to nudge us back into the fiery pit as revenge for our disturbing their awe-inspiring cosiness. For the adult world gardens have a fatal image, as damning and damned as cake decoration. A circle of hell – but some of us are determined to try to escape and some people can just about see us waving.

ROSES AND TASTE

I like the idea of bad plants but I'm not sure they really exist. Well, I can think of *one*: the rose.

THE ROSE

We are all aware of roses; our culture and our history are saturated with them. For most people they epitomize beauty and romance and I won't bore you with telling you all about why, when and where. Enough people have done that. We are told that the garden world shook in horror and shock when Christopher Lloyd removed the roses from his rose garden. I take that with a lot of salt and detect rather the relish that the garden media world felt having a story with a slight air of novelty which combined the key words 'Lloyd' and 'roses'. But it does indicate the place that roses are believed to hold in gardeners' minds and the ubiquity of rose gardens. And, after all, why not? Roses can be stupendous.

I love ramblers. I love the posh, stilted roses that pack an amazing scent when they are in a vase, looking sophisticated. I love 'Felicia' and many of the shrubby, robust roses (hybrid musk in this case) like her. I love three rose gardens in season. The wonderful Moor Wood in Woodmancote (love the name too), Gloucestershire, specializes in throwing both monstrous and well-behaved ramblers – in fact ramblers of every kind – all over the vertical surfaces of a small green valley, principally over the walls of extensive terraces, making them rather more accessible than mine. Mine climb up trees and over the garage.

I also know of two other great rose gardens: David Austin Roses, Albrighton, the showplace for the English roses bred there, and Mottisfont Abbey in Romsey,

Hampshire. Mottisfont, designed by Graham Stuart Thomas, has rose gardens to die for (odd expression but conjures up the right picture of fainting away from total ecstasy – of the original kind) and is full of his much-loved shrub roses as well as some of the very best of everything else, selected by someone who knew roses. What do these two have in common? They are lavish. Roses are it. They are romantic, generous, well designed, colour conscious, the sun always shines, underplanted, healthy . . . Well, yes, I guess you get the picture. Go and look if you can, and yearn if you can't.

But elsewhere in the world you find that the worst thing in the garden world is roses. Big blobs stuck up on the end of long, prickly bare stems, usually in bare soil with the odd sad weed straggling into the picture and often in garish, contrasting, ill-mixed colours. 'Lovely,' the punters say, 'lovely.'

How come? What do they see? Have they

OPPOSITE *Rosa* 'Felicia' – a reliable, gorgeous hybrid musk with fewer off days than most roses.
RIGHT *Rosa* 'Paul's Himalayan Musk' – a huge rambler. What trees are for.

had a kind of Pavlovian training? Instead of salivating at the sight of dog food they've been trained to salivate at the sight of sticky-up roses? I cannot believe they are actually *looking* at what is in front of them. Really looking. I visited Bodnant recently, and there, on the rose terrace was a blooming example of that worst kind – mixed colours, many looking diseased and defoliated despite having been planted quite recently. There was a board at the entrance to the garden telling me what was looking good that day. And it was headlined with the – yes, quite – the rose terrace.

What was looking good at Bodnant that day, but not mentioned, was tree trunks. The form and shape of trees, many with trunks bared to show off their beauty of their lines, are wonderfully displayed at Bodnant: it's a bit like, good stems = trees, awful stems = roses. If you got your eye in for the good I believe you'd be ripping the bad out in no time.

This issue of ugly roses brought up a challenging idea and a perhaps entertaining story. I visited the rose circle at Spetchley Park, Worcestershire, with the great nurseryman Bob Brown. Bob is great company – combative, challenging, entertaining – and writes a great plant catalogue. We stood together looking at this sad ring of roses, classic blobs on sticks, and he said he loved them.

With most garden types that would be the end of it. It would be no good asking why because they would resent the very question and you certainly wouldn't get a coherent answer. But our Bob is different, so I asked, 'Why do you love them?'

And he replied: 'Because they are historic in this place; because I love roses and because the cognoscenti [that's me, folks] don't like them.' What is noticeable about this answer is that none of those reasons had anything to do with what we were actually looking at and the experience of looking at them. They were all thoughts, ideas, notions. And it rapidly became apparent that experience of any kind was not likely to impinge on these notions.

But I had a problem in attempting to open his eyes, and that was that I couldn't get beyond the word 'ugly' myself. I couldn't find any way of communicating that ugliness or, indeed, justifying it, in the company of someone who could not or would not see it, even though it was shouting at me.

I have thought long and hard about this problem, which I think amounts to: 'Why do we, as human beings, find some things intrinsically beautiful?' Of course this is arguable, and people go on about differences in taste, but I believe that those of us I know most about, Europeans, very largely share some overall preference for certain kinds of views and things to look at.

There is considerable argument about why this may be the case. It used to be popular among garden professionals – lecturers, writers – to argue that it is because human beings 'grew up' in a savannah-type environment and so evolved with a preference for something safe at the back and an open landscape in front, with little groups of trees to run and hide in when admiring the view is interrupted by the arrival of a sabre-toothed tiger.

This view, however appealing, seems to be discredited as over-simplified. And clearly it doesn't tell us why we might like a rose. But there does seem to be something which needs explaining. I've noticed that when I come across something beautiful I register instant pleasure – instantly: far too fast to be a judgement arrived at by consideration or thinking about. I recently had the good fortune to stay in a cottage in the grounds of a good garden (Plas Cadnant on Anglesey). The view from my bedroom window was down a particular section of the garden, and every time I caught sight of it in passing my spirits lifted. Immediately, as if some part of me was just saying 'Yes!'

And I have to say I seem to have as swift a reaction of 'No' far more often.

It is clear that not everyone would have just this reaction. And I have been focused on looking at gardens for about thirty years, so I am not your man in the street. But the reaction is so visceral that I believe in it.

I have recently read that a preference for certain music is 'hardwired' into the brain. Journalist Hannah Devlin reports that Dr Kikuchi, a physiologist from the University of Georgetown, believes she has found out why certain sounds seem right to us: 'We have a very innate musical perception – even an infant can perceive an octave.' She goes on to discuss the physical basis for this possibility, and for the direct link to the emotions which music has. Although it is early days for this science, it echoes my own intuitive sense that the pleasure we find in scent, sights and sounds goes deep. But the variation in the way we appreciate those things suggests that there is, as always, a subtle and complex interplay between this and acquired responses.

We do, after all, develop a great deal of mind clutter when we are young. Most children are taught at a very early age what to appreciate. They are offered a flower, invited to sniff it and told, 'Pretty, Freddie, pretty.' And if you doubt that these early lessons persist try offering a flower to anyone. The odds are that unless they are a botanical artist their first reaction will be to sniff it. And then, probably, admire it. They will do this even if the flower is made of silk or for some other reason is totally scentless.

We are also taught at a formative age not to put our hands in the fire or run across a road without looking, and these useful lessons stay with us for life – under the age of five we are primed to 'introject', that is, to swallow ideas whole and undigested and then hang on to them for life. It is possible to shed these ideas, but it is a long, painstaking process.

But it is also possible to refine these introjects – polish them, as it were. So that an inclination to like 'gardens' or 'roses', on account of having been told early on that these were beautiful, may begin under the exposure to many, many gardens and many, many roses to become 'I prefer this garden/this rose to that one.' This is the development of what we call 'taste' and discrimination. We know well that wine tasters do this, but people are sometimes reluctant to accept that garden tasters develop skill in taste and discrimination too, preferring to believe that 'It's just personal taste,' as if a wine taster has not developed a 'nose' but just has random, indiscriminate preferences. Or that a garden taster – well, hopefully you get my point.

So I believe that constant refinement can rid our minds of some of the garden clutter. With a little effort, and the inclination (which is no doubt totally lacking), Bob Brown could study roses over a few years, admiring them in bud, in blossom and in decay; on bushes, on stalks, in vases and buttonholes; in rose circles, rose gardens and up trees. He could grow them, prune them, care for them and dig them up and throw them away. (But not sell them, because this would add a totally different concern – how commercial?) And, critically, he could confront the notion that 'All roses are lovely.' He could, furthermore, ask himself whether he is old and wise enough to use his own judgement rather than simply form his judgements on disliking that which he believes the cognoscenti approve of. And begin to wonder whether historical authenticity is enough to justify the inclusion of roses in a particular garden in a particular place.

And at that point interesting and enlightening discussion can take place.

This is a good model too for learning to be discriminating about gardens, and I do so wish lots of people would. It would be a much more interesting and exciting world to inhabit and soon we would begin to have more really exciting gardens.

WATER MAINTENANCE

Water is as hard to look after in the garden as grass. It requires constant maintenance – and, unlike with grass, there are few machines offering help. Surprisingly a great many gardens of the kind that trim their edges and keep their grass meticulously don't bother about their water. Large areas of sludgy green algae frequently swamp the surface of pools and ponds (what is the difference between a pool and a pond?), which should ideally be at least largely clean and reflective: that is what water does for a garden. Sludgy algae are the worst, but rampant water lily sometimes does the same obscuring act. I don't really understand this neglect, except that algae are so hard to get rid of and the getting rid of never seems to be entirely satisfactory.

Blanket weed, the worst in appearance perhaps, can be hauled out by the barrowload and you'll never get the last little bit. You know it will be back in a week. Well, so will the grass growth, but heaving out weed is not quite the same as driving round on a mini tractor and the result is not as satisfying. The proliferation of products which are supposed to remove blanket weed proves the extent of the problem. When something has a cure, it has a cure. And that one cure is what is available. It's all that is needed, after all. If there is no real cure there will also be five hundred claimed cures and none of them will work satisfactorily.

The dismal green sheet depresses me and it adheres determinedly to the edge of the pool. I spend quite some time every summer removing it with a rake or just pulling it out by hand, but I can never get all of it and I can never detach it from its tenacious hold on the side – it holds on like a terrified and stubborn child refusing to try swimming. There is no entirely satisfactory tool for the job. I use a rake mostly. Sometimes a piece of rough wood. But if you have an implement that the weed will cling to, it will *continue* to cling and have to be pulled off the implement by hand.

Duckweed is as irremovable when it has taken hold, though much prettier, being a bright, cheerful shade of green. It looks quite innocent at first and the unwary might even welcome it as an attractive pond-shading assistant. But it spreads like duckweed.

Designers at garden festivals have been known to take advantage of its

Lemna minor (lesser duckweed) and mirrors arranged in a chequerboard pattern at Chaumont Garden Festival. Now that's better than a load of grey-green algae. Designers J.M. Desgrolard, J.M. Blanchet, J. Dufour.

attractiveness and use it in controlled patterns on water, divided up by batons and the like. As always, creating a pattern displays intention and helps convert from weed to design, and some of the results have been wonderful. The maintenance involved in containing the weed to its allotted space is a challenge. But it could be worth considering in a small garden as an alternative to digging out the roots of bindweed or turning the compost heap: so much more satisfying, and the result well worth the effort, unlike the aforementioned soulless activities.

If you have running water in a 'water feature' (it's amazing that we cannot find a better expression than this: fountain is better, but if it dribbles water is that really the right term?), the algae will arrange itself differently, dripping globbily down the face of a stainless-steel surface, for example, but it will still appear.

We made a trip to a local farm once for a bale of barley straw and tolerated being clearly regarded as bonkers by the farmer. Well, quite right, for all the good it did after a lot of embarrassment, problem-solving (how to transport? administer? store?) and work.

I have returned to physical removal and scrubbing (of our fountain).

The most critical area of water we have to keep clear is the reflecting pool. If we have unexpected visitors this is where you'll find me fleeing to with a fishing net.

The whole beauty of the pool can be, and frequently is, destroyed by a variety of unpleasantnesses. Of which algae are only one, and in this context the easiest. The reflecting pool is designed to have nothing growing in it, and so all growing things are removed. No fish, no plants, no frogs. So a drop of bleach does wonders. (No, not against frogs. They and their spawn get lifted out and removed to the other pool). Even, so far, for the first few leaves of duckweed . . .

But bigger leaves are different and have to be fished out, so the autumn can be challenging. Though just sometimes a few leaves can add a certain something. Especially in rich autumn colour, before they go soggy, brown and depressing. And they are easy-ish to fish out. Tree seeds are not. These plague posh pools at the Chelsea Flower Show, where trees are energetically spreading their seeds around at just the wrong moment for the designers. The seeds will be tiny – can even be mistaken for a kind of algae – and very disfiguring to the water surface. But there is a good trick for dealing with these, and it is for this you have stayed the course, tolerated my depressing messages about algaecides, grimaced past my hard-work remedies; this one is not hard work, or difficult, and can be totally transforming in a matter of minutes. A garden sprinkler – preferably of the waft-waft kind rather than one of the spinning ones – played on the pool for ten minutes (filling it up at the same time if needed) will clear the surface miraculously. If any bits remain you will find them at the edge, easy to net out.

I imagine it works by breaking up the surface tension which keeps these fine particles suspended on the water – that or the sheer force of water droplets on the bits. Heavy rain does the same trick – the pool looks wonderful after a thunderstorm. Best trick in the book, that.

The other major contribution to the pleasure of water is gradually becoming known now, and it is another miracle. I had not considered, when I had the pool made, and made just six inches deep, just how the reflections would be created. I kind of thought that a black lining would do it. It didn't. The black lining is not black enough; every crease and irregularity on its surface catches light and reflects light back to the now glum viewer. As the new pool fills you are confronted by the fact that water is, well, transparent. You can see the bits of gravel and dirt on the bottom, the dead slugs and the yew clippings.

Since we had invested more in the promise of reflections than we had ever spent anywhere else in the garden this failure was not to be countenanced. I had to colour up the water. I tried to find dyes and discovered, as is often the case, that I was after something no one else wanted, or that no one else had thought of. You could get *blue* to make your pool look like the transplanted Mediterranean, but not black. I tried ink. Went nowhere – I would have needed gallons and gallons of the stuff. Food dye. Again – made no impression. Paint stain! That did it. It was hard to find, because, of course, people like to paint their fences orange or imitation wood colours, not black (fools). But when I got it, the black wood stain worked. It was probably illegal. It didn't last a season without fading, but it was affordable and I bought it like a junkie.

Until I discovered an organic black dye. I had to import it from America at great expense, but it took only a tiny amount to colour the pool and it was designed for the job. They use it in lakes there; don't know precisely what for (to hide the fish from predators?).

My six-inch-deep pool now looks bottomless. I am asked about how this trick is done more than anything else in the garden. I love putting it in to a freshly filled pool (I clean it out every spring).

Miracle.

ERIGERON KARVINSKIANUS 'PROFUSION'

Some ideas are so good they become ubiquitous, and erigeron scattered around everywhere in paving is one of them. It flowers continuously, eagerly seeds itself and comes readily from seed so just lends itself to this use. There are some gardens with vast slabs of terracing looking quite bleak and unwelcoming, but erigeron can help soften things up. It might also make an attractive edging to a path.

You can spread it, or let it spread itself, in lots of odd corners that might otherwise be dull or weedy. Buy some seed today and then look for places to pop it in. One of the very few plants you can work this way round with (instead of knowing where it's going before you get it).

So it's useful, quite pretty. And then after a while it goes background. One of those furnishing plants that we all should have, like ferns, honesty and valerian in walls and odd corners. Unless you're stark, modern and clean.

The terrace sprinkled with *Erigeron karvinskianus* 'Profusion' and with *Stipa tenuissima* just beginning to spread. *Campanula portenschlagiana* scrambles over the walls.

SHOW GARDENS

I can't quite get show gardens. I find it hard to look at them, hard to take them in, hard to make sense of them or in any way to relate to them. (Especially when, six months before they exist, garden articles invite the press to 'view some of the innovative gardens at this year's flower show'. I'm not joking.)

I go along to Chelsea or some similar event with 'show gardens' and love seeing all my colleagues and having a good gossip. But I find it hard to find anything intelligent to say about the gardens. Which is why I have begun to prefer reporting other people's comments rather than my own.

It's not that they are temporary, or even that perhaps you can't get into them. You certainly can't get in to a garden at Chelsea unless you're being filmed or being especially shown round because you're a friend of the designer. Unless you're very pushy. But I've found the same at the shows that do let you in, as Westonbirt and Future Gardens did – they leave me with the same non-reaction. I look and look and it is as if I am seeing nothing. A thing, in effect, which has no resonance, though it might be stunning to look at.

I know it sounds strange and precious, and it's hard to understand. No one else seems to be having that problem, judging by the millions of words that come out about Chelsea gardens, often before they're even built. But if I am in what I am forced to call, for want of a better term – though I hate it – a 'real' garden the problem simply isn't there. Why?

Well, I had to get there, to a 'real' garden – in other words this is a destination. I have been through some kind of context which has narrowed itself down from a city, or a countryside, a something, until it is this particular place. And maybe whatever the overdone 'sense of place' is (a sense of *a* place maybe?) this is it. A show garden is next door to another show garden and another and another – how to really focus? And they are all in something/somewhere else, which tends not to be especially related or connected to this show garden, and sometimes is downright oppressive (Chelsea) or ugly (Future Gardens 2009). A real garden has a context and how it relates to that context is part of whether it works or not. The context contributes to its particularity.

In Swansea there is a back street amid a mass of ordinary street housing, and in that back street a gate. You open the gate and step into a magical transformation:

The Ridler Garden, Swansea. A view across the kitchen garden with apple 'Queen Cox' in the foreground and *Buxus sempervirens* 'Pyramidalis' echoing the shape of the obelisks.

a topiary garden. Having your head in one before the other is part of the delight. And there the domestic ordinariness keeps slipping back in – round the edges, and in the form of the compost heap . . . The garden (the Ridler garden) never entirely escapes the world around it; you are not 'transported' so much as thrown into dramatic juxtaposition.

A garden I visited last year is reached down a narrow country lane and as you stand with your back to a meadow you face a classic country cottage with bouncy box hedges overfilling their spaces. Maybe a house is a vital part of the difference? Well, you might think that but the Ridler garden hasn't really got one (it has an office but it really doesn't offer the focus and centre that a house usually does). But both these gardens engage with the world they are part of, and perhaps a show garden by its very nature is not engaging with its world, just sitting in it for a time.

Most gardens of any size manage to offer a journey, a genuine route of discovery – both the above gardens do. But I cannot think of a Chelsea garden I have ever seen which offers that, though sometimes they claim to. The reason? You are never, because of the necessity to offer viewing from the sides, really in it, never enclosed, and your destination is always visible.

And then, 'real' gardens get lived in. I don't mean by that that they have dustbins and barbecues – some show gardens have those. I mean that someone, for good or ill, gardens them continuously. They have evolved. Parts of them are having an off day; some parts may shine. Whoever is responsible for them gets a long go at fiddling with them, adjusting, changing, keeping at it. They remain a work in progress. They don't arrive fresh off a drawing board. Not like a show garden. The show garden looks like a confection, an illusion, a phantom.

Given all those advantages, you would think we could do a lot better than we do in our 'private' gardens, wouldn't you?

THE CONSERVATORY

You may not quote this back at me when and if I leave this garden, overwhelmed by grief. But I think it's possible that if I only had a conservatory or an equivalent space to play with, together with a back-up area – a greenhouse or simply a hidden space – then I could possibly play in peace and pleasure for the rest of my life. This is the best game, the conservatory – and the most expensive. Lots of shopping. Lots of instant gratification. If you have only a small, sad garden, listen up.

It hasn't always been like this. I started the way I imagine everyone starts if they have the great good fortune to acquire a conservatory. I thought it was for tender plants. Especially scented climbers. I bought specimens of all the lovely things I could now grow and sort of put them around the place. They were mostly perennial so they sat there, sometimes for years, getting rather tatty and boring. One day Charles asked me to get rid of them.

Echeveria runyonii 'Topsy Turvy' in the conservatory.

I was a bit shocked, but could see he was right. So here are the first two rules for stylish conservatory owners. 1. Don't get preoccupied with tender plants: get preoccupied with *good* plants. 2. Throw them away when they don't look *brilliant* any more. This is a place where they really have to pull their weight. It's no good thinking they'll suddenly perk up and wow you. They won't. Ever. And, anyway, you've got bored and dispirited looking at them.

This is why you need a spare area. If you insist on tender plants it will have to be a greenhouse. But I really think it's best to be more liberal in your choices. Tender plants are not necessarily the most telling. If the plants are hardy, a nursery area will do and will have your plants-in-waiting in the fresh air, even in the frost. And all that will help keep the pests down.

I have to contend with one of the very worst pests, so I know of what we speak. I have a monster red spider mite, vigorous and visible to the naked eye, running up and down the leaves and making depressing webs everywhere. I have tried everything, including things I shouldn't have, and they come back cocky as ever, whatever. I've poisoned, steamed, wiped, washed – mostly doing more harm to the plants than the pest. I never get rid of it, but a holiday outside for a tormented plant often seems to free it up for a while and return it to health. Hence my preference for hardy plants – I like to think of the bugs getting frozen out there in the winter, global warming permitting.

What plants, then? Well, maybe anything as long as on the whole you don't buy them in singles. Singles is sad, several is good. As always: think repeat, think pattern. I discovered that these pests of mine (I sometimes think the conservatory is actually a conservation area for extra-big red spider mites) don't seem fond of succulents. But I am: they make super shapes. They come in some good colours, are sculptural in their own right and, repeated, make patterns. They rarely look identical for long, but if they do when you buy them then exploit that aspect and put them prominently together. They get the table treatment in our house – stage centre and before us as we eat. Then they start to show idiosyncrasy: one will wave a flower at you, another grow a baby at its side. This becomes a different pleasure, though not quite so much an 'in your face' pleasure. Windowsill is good, then, to admire the repetition laced with variety. To flower or not? Personally I wish they wouldn't, but Charles likes some of the flowers so I tolerate them for a while. Then take enormous pleasure in chopping all the stalks off, flowers and all, and see pure sculpture re-emerge supreme. (He never notices.)

No need to grow succulents, though. What wouldn't work? I suggested growing roses in ours. Charles told me that was crazy, but, then, maybe . . . because look at the virtues. You could have them on display only when they were vigorously in flower (as long as they didn't have stalky, prickly legs). You get flower, colour and

ABOVE Staging with agave, cannas, ferns, and succulents. *Sansevieria trifasciata*, mother-in-law's tongue, is supposed to be indestructible. I managed to destruct.
OPPOSITE *Cyperus alternifolius*, umbrella plant, sitting permanently in water in zinc-plated containers.

scent. If they get greenfly or (they will) red spider you simply shove them out back into the nursery until they've learnt to cope. I'll try it one year.

And this is the big treat: changing the look every couple of months. That way you see it all again freshly, find yourself looking forward to getting up in the morning to go and have another look.

Bulbs in the spring – this is the way to grow tulips. Fill your conservatory (or a windowsill?): a row of three or five or seven pots. (It doesn't have to be odd numbers actually; just fill the available space well. The odd numbers thing may be a gardener's superstition.) Try something else in between them, maybe – find what you have to hand that will set them off. Or off to the garden centre again for just the right thing: ferns, maybe?

Oh, windowsills. I once had a London flat with a large kitchen window facing a blank wall. We shelved it with toughened glass shelves, all the way up the window, and filled the shelves with plants. (Um, downside? Had to climb into the sink to water them.)

You can see how this is a perfect recipe for a small garden. Pave it over, make

your seating and eating area and then create some stylish staging to bring things up to eye level and above, where they show off best and save you from bending down. Stick your bins underneath. Get a lot of cachepots to help show the plants off, in a variety of sizes. Metal or plastic waste paper bins are worth considering: punch holes in the bottom for those plants that don't enjoy sitting in water, or – good trick – raise them off the floor of the pot with a bit of brick, bits of broken tile or similar, so that they drain and don't sit in the wet. Or buy plants which love water and naturally sit in it, put in pots with no holes and only worry about them in a drought – reeds, cannas . . . This is a really useful idea. Overwatering ceases to be a worry: just keep topping up generously. Much easier than trying to hold off as you have to with succulents. Voice of experience. Paint the staging a colour that you love and which sets your plants off. And don't forget a small nursery area concealed somewhere if you can find the space. Then play.

But do be ruthless. This is not the motley mixed-pot collection you're doing. We've seen it, we've hated it, we don't want it. You're going for stunning not messing. So go for it and chuck out what doesn't look great.

I ended up painting our conservatory black. I love black. It sets the plants off so well and the galvanized cachepots look good against it too. It felt a bit radical. We'd already painted the woodwork of the conservatory and house black, to help the house itself disappear into the background. It's an ugly house, a mad mix of old cottage and barn with 1960s extension and a garage block that's even worse.

So the conservatory had its black beginnings. The walls felt like a bigger step. So I painted one wall and we looked at it for a summer. Looked good. So I did the rest and we love it. Favourite place. In the world? Maybe. Well, reflecting pool? (And it leaks, unlike the reflecting pool.)

So do think beyond the ubiquitous white: there are so many more exciting colours which are also kinder to live with. The blue white that is so popular in paint is harshest of all; if you like white consider a creamy white. Or consider a whole colour scheme and base the colour of your walls – or fences, if it is a garden – on that. Red flowers against a deep grey-green? Yellows against blue – or vice versa? (Harder – there are fewer true blue flowers than yellow ones.) Concentrate on a foliage colour and try every variety of that which is generally called purple against orange? The excitements are legion and all that it would take to change the whole lot would be a paintbrush and plant sale, followed by more plant shopping. (Give up the foreign holidays.)

Strangely, there is no need, apparently, to be rigid in the application of colour through the whole scheme. I have a blue table and terracotta tile floor, which adds two colours to the silver and black, in addition to the inevitable green of some foliage that I use. But I find they harmonize. It's the same as with creating borders: trial and error and keep looking.

When I add tulips in spring any gaudy colour may appear: that's the whole point of tulips. Apart from elegance, of course. I think it all works because they are the only really bright colours there; the more subdued colours around then set them off. But if they didn't look good when they came out I could find space in the house for them.

I filled the conservatory with petunias one year. Annuals are good for this kind of treatment and it's getting easier to get them in single colours so that you can maximize the drama. Whitefly killed that off for me, but you might be luckier – as long as you never import a single one of the horrors. If you do, give up quick. Total abstinence from susceptible plants after total throw-out of infected ones is the only way to stay sane and go on enjoying your plants. I persisted in trying to get rid of them for years and it was a waste of my time and spirit. Be brave. There are lots of other things to try that are less susceptible. Soft-leaved flowering plants are the most attractive to them, I believe.

Having been forced to give up on many of the flowers for the time being – though having got whitefly-free (fingers crossed) I may yet try again – I have focused on good leaf. Cannas, phormiums, melianthus (whitefly-prone, though – I cannot now see one without turning the leaf to check), astelia and grasses. Other possibilities would be hostas: here is your chance to keep them slug-free. There are big ones, full of elegance, like 'Krossa Regal', or there are miniatures to contrast maybe with your succulents. Try clipped box if you have space. Or purple fennel for contrast to your hostas. Once you lose the straitjacket of 'tender' the world is full of wonderful possibilities.

Useful tip: keep a compost bin in there. It makes life so much easier if you can instantly dispose of dead leaves, weeds (it's a bit much weeding pots, but if the plants spend any time outdoors you can bet your life the weeds will find them) and apple cores when you're having a sit and a nibble. I use a galvanized dustbin, which fits the scheme, but has to sit in a discreet plant tray because it has begun to leak valuable compost liquids.

I feed plants when I repot, with long-lasting fertilizer pellets. It's almost like a superstition – I have no idea how necessary it is. I have sometimes failed to feed a plant for a long time and begun to wonder if all this emphasis on plant food is overdone. It is impossible to experiment with everything in the garden, so I have never systematically fed and unfed plants to discover the truth about how much plant food any kind of plant may need, but I am aware that it is another of those things which garden writers endlessly repeat without much evidence of their own. This winter I had some cyclamen, which had been sitting in pouring rain outside all summer, presumably any fertilizer having been washed totally away, cheerfully and spontaneously start flowering. I repot somewhat randomly and sometimes find to my surprise that some plants manage very well with no fresh compost and just having their roots cut off as they grow out of the pots. This is not to recommend any of this terrible delinquent behaviour, just to encourage a healthy scepticism and spirit of enquiry.

DEADHEADING

I just deadheaded a day lily and accidentally took a new bud off with it. I never usually deadhead, and now I remember why. I know, or at least I am reliably informed, that deadheading is good. Helps to build up the vigour of the plant, preventing it putting resources into producing seed. Unless the seed heads are important, of course, in which case all that can, rather oddly, go hang. We are similarly told to water outdoor plants thoroughly so as to prevent the roots coming up for the water. But no one ever tells you to rush out after a slight shower to water the garden in order to keep those foolish roots in the right place, do they?

Anyway, I find deadheading slightly problematic. Principally because we've got too many plants that would demand it of us if we started listening (this is why we lose marks for maintenance). So, apart from pinching a dead flower off with my finger and thumb sometimes in passing, I tend to ignore the problem. I'm most likely to wait till it's all over and cut the lot down with the hedge-trimmer.

Or pull them out in the case of willowherb. Total removal can then make what is coming on behind visible: it's a good trick to have tall things flowering at the front, with other things which are later flowering behind. Then chop chop after the front row has stopped flowering and the next layer is revealed, ready to perform. Magic. Though it may be sensible to leave as much of the plant below the flowering stem as possible, to help it build up for next year's display: so whereas I remove the ordinary rosebay willowherb completely, I only cut the tops off the hybrids.

But deadheading to keep things going? Like a day lily? Question is, if it involves that much faffing do you ever get to enjoy it? No, because when you return to that spot several days later it looks just the same as when you first started. I have sometimes suddenly recollected that I'd deadheaded something and wondered what it looked like afterwards – whether it actually did flower again – because I'd totally forgotten about it. All this is no doubt different in a small garden, but then so is most gardening.

Sometimes I have an hour by myself in an evening and get drawn outside, to plant something or cut a small area of hedge – something gentle, effective and which focuses my attention on a small area of the garden. It's called pottering – some people call it gardening – and it's very pleasant. I guess deadheading is like that for some people.

GRASSES

These are frequently described as fashionable. What's wrong with 'fashionable', I asked in the *Garden Design Journal* and Jill Billington replied, 'Simply, overuse.'

Are grasses overused? I may be seeing the wrong gardens – I'm sure I am, since garden designers and judges for the RHS must be exposed to very different gardens than those of us who are largely confined to visiting 'gardens open to the public'. I also, perhaps, have a different frame of reference. I do sometimes become painfully aware of the different worlds we all function in and how strangely that must affect our understanding of each other. A friend yesterday told me about a 'gardening quiz' on the radio and suggested (although she described it as terribly boring) that I should listen to it. I would no more listen to a 'gardening quiz' than I would go deep sea diving, that is only on pain of death, but because I'm identified as a 'gardener' that is the perspective people have on my interests in the world.

I'm not sure if I can communicate how bizarre it feels being lumped into a group of people who might like to listen to a gardening quiz – or presumably, watch *Gardeners' World*. It's a bit like being offered a Noddy book because you are reputed to be interested in English literature. It may have its own bizarre interest, as a kind of curiosity or phenomenon, but it's not quite what I'd choose.

There doesn't seem to be a grown-up image of gardens, or indeed gardeners, in the public mind. We are either eccentric middle-aged ladies, getting off on the excitement of watching Toby Buckland with his spade, or hoary-handed sons of toil (who on earth were they?).

To the point: I have not, in my part of the garden world, been overexposed yet to grasses. I do still see them occasionally in that naïve and uncomprehending abortion, the 'grasses border', where they are lumped together like those of us interested in gardens, without discrimination. We and they may somehow have strayed into the same class of things, but we don't do well, or look right, shoved all together indiscriminately.

I believe that grasses look best as a brilliant addition to late borders, as seen to great effect in several German parks, or in blocks of a single variety, adding that wonderful sculptural effect which blocks of hedges also offer. They can look wonderful in both contexts. I use them in both ways, the latter more successfully than the former at present, I believe.

The grasses border is situated on a small hillside, which means both that there is a view from the top of it, which is the highest point of the garden, and also that it is visible from the opposite side of the valley. This creates design problems and opportunities. One of the problems was that any planting needed to be low enough to see over; shrubs or trees would have effectively obscured the view out of the garden, and that view is one of the delights of the place for me. It has to be attained: in other words, you don't see it every day. My friends used to have a stunning view over the Usk valley, which we loved to enjoy when we visited. But they saw it whenever they looked out of the window and it had clearly lost its savour. Having to go outside and climb a hill to enjoy a view is not too arduous but does give it a comparatively refreshing scarcity.

The fact that you can see the planting from the opposite hillside is clearly an opportunity and a challenge, and it proved incredibly difficult to achieve the effect I wanted.

The obvious solution was to go for a flat 'prairie' planting, or a version of it – a large area with large and telling sweeps of herbaceous planting. But this seemed

BELOW The grasses parterre, with *Phalaris arundinacea* 'Feesey', *Stipa gigantea* and *Pleioblastus viridistriatus*. I love the cleaned-up tree trunks in the background: I don't think we show trees off like this often enough.
OPPOSITE A view across the grasses parterre to the countryside beyond, caught in beautiful light. In the foreground, *P.a.* 'Feesey'.

wrong. Alien to a (relatively) small garden in the Wye Valley. Alien to my aim of acknowledging the essence of the place and its history. For a long time I was stuck.

Then, as I have recounted elsewhere, I did a 'Mary' and sat around with a glass of wine on a holiday in France while friends made our supper. Sitting dozily drinking I had the critical flash of possibility: a planting of grasses within the 1841 tithe map. This was right in every way: practical – it was low; aesthetic – it would have pattern and movement, and would look good close to and from across the valley; and emblematic – it would pay homage to the landscape and history of the land itself.

So far so good. The next bit was many years of expense and struggle. Without doubt this was and is the hardest part of the garden to make. The box plants outlining the field boundaries (a challenge in themselves to translate on to the ground) had to be tiny, as that was all I could afford, and I planted them at a very wide spacing. This would have worked elsewhere in the garden but this slope was problematic. I have never been able to work out how wet or dry it actually is. Near the top the hedgerow with fully mature trees dries the soil for an amazing distance – I discover tree roots where reason would tell you no tree roots should be. But water from the whole of the ridge above us drains away through this land and I believe I have lost plants more from rotting than cold.

The box has survived so far, but I ended up adding plants in between the originals when I could afford it because towards the top it was drier and more challenged and they were so slow growing. I started out with them a yard apart

and then eighteen inches. After many years the ones at the top of the slope have still to join up properly in hedge formation. Meanwhile it's kind of 'join the dots'. And we have box disease in the garden, so there is a constant background anxiety about this irreplaceable hedging. We could never afford any of the possible alternatives.

I grew the grasses initially from seed and, as usual, had no real idea what they would be like apart from written descriptions. My initial rule was that they had to grow below three feet tall so as not to obscure the pattern of hedges, but I have recently introduced *Stipa gigantea*. The height of the flowers is immaterial, given how airy and unobscuring the flower stems are. I had a great many failures – quite apart from anything else the rabbits ate them. Planting out thirty or forty plants grown painstakingly from seed, only to have them eaten, was one of the biggest heartbreaks in making the garden and resulted in Charles spending a whole winter rabbit-fencing the garden. Which was great – after we'd got rid of the rabbits which got trapped inside.

Then I had winter losses. And I came to the conclusion that our knowledge of grasses in this country was rather limited. They are often described as 'easy' and 'trouble-free', but this was very far from my experience. I even had whole sections of bought-in plants fail, after I had got affluent enough to buy some occasionally. £100 dead – no joke.

Increasingly I used the same grasses, ones which had already proved themselves survivors with me, in several different places. There were other reasons than their survival for this: the second major problem was how they read from across the valley.

This was critical and terrible. I'd get a section established and spend a year or more looking at it growing (they had to fill out a lot to make a judgement valid), only to be forced to the conclusion that it didn't read clearly enough, or that the colour didn't work in relation to the colours around it.

I went for subtle originally and then decided that contrast was really important if the pattern was to declare itself clearly enough. This meant introducing yellows (grasses became bamboos, *Pleioblastus viridistriatus*) and white stripes (*Phalaris arundinacea* 'Feesey'.) These were good and vigorous – and induced horror in Piet Oudolf when he visited. I think this pointed up our different worlds. He can presumably choose his plants solely on the basis of their suitability, aesthetically and culturally, since he can afford as many as are required to fill a space. I need to consider plants which will also fill that space for me from as few plants as possible. The price I pay is the risk of their spreading beyond my ability to cope – and, who knows? They may yet do just that. But along with their ability to spread tends to come an ability to survive once established – double bonus. So I take the risk.

Stipa gigantea flowers for months, with the vertical of the flowers echoing the vertical tree trunks.

Some grasses, such as *Anemanthele lessoniana*, were supposed to be robust and 'prolific self-seeders'. Maybe, but they didn't reappear until very late spring, resulting in repeated despairing trips up the hill to inspect, and when they did reappear they had succeeded in dying out in patches. (The expert on grasses Roger Grounds tells me that he believes this is a grass which prefers not to be cut down at all.) *Stipa tenuifolia* did no better but had me hoping for longer. If you manage weeds by mulching it is simply no good to look for plants to replace themselves by self-seeding. If you defeat seeding weeds, you defeat seeding plants, and that's it.

So this part of the garden has been a long time coming. But now it nearly has, I love it and it does as I imagined. It has a very long life of looking good, spring being the only off time, as the grasses are mostly cut down then. Though the pattern of the hedges is now nearly there and that is year-round. I love the (successful) grasses close to, too, so this planting takes me from one side of the garden – the long view – to the other – the near view. From either side the pattern of yew hedges in the bottom looks stunning.

So grasses, fashionable or not, seem indispensable to me. Perfect for windy gardens and for creating pattern, contrast and structure. Beautiful in winter. Often sensuous to touch – though can be dagger sharp too, so beware.

PLANTING STYLE
AT THE VEDDW

Planting according to colour has slipped off the fashion map recently with the move towards 'prairie planting', alias flat planting, with mixes of colour relieved by grasses. This meadow influence has spread into fashionable borders which have consequently lost their preoccupations with varying heights, ins and outs, and offering a variety of shapes and form. At least the fashionable border owners have. This is probably not really very widespread and my thoughts are possibly influenced by a lot of exposure to designer gardens and pictures of designer gardens. Having just done a bit of garden visiting I notice that in the majority of gardens we have never actually left the last century and most gardens have not actually yet *arrived* at considering colour much when planting.

Cardoons (*Cynara cardunculus* 'Florist Cardy') and box egg cups – sadly struggling with the ravages of box blight, but still surviving.

Either way what I seem to see very little of, while rejoicing in it at the Veddw, is using colour dramatically. Walking round the garden this morning, on a miserable wet late August day after a miserable wet summer, I found my spirits lifted by turning a corner to find massed blue and yellow smacking me in the face. I then turned the corner into the veg plot to see the silver cardoons with their grounding of purple-brown heuchera set against the same colours in the background of shrubs – and the whole lifted into delight by the various shades of pink from massed anemones.

And reflecting on the gardens I have visited recently I'd say that what marks these dramas out is not just sticking to a colour theme but also, and critically, not mixing up lots of different plants, even ones which are in the right colour range. I know that sticking with a particular colour range is one way of allowing yourself to succumb to the temptation to buy plants at every opportunity, but the best effect is actually achieved by repetition, it really is. Christopher Lloyd was well known for so-say daring colour schemes but when I revisit pictures of Great Dixter I find the muddle an irritant to my eye. If I were to replant the Veddw, and I may have to one day, to make it manageable in our old age, I would simplify further than I have done.

A gesture in the direction of the wow factor is repetition of single plants. I visited Tintinhull last week and there are several small borders with a single repeated plant. Pleasing, very pleasing. Maybe not wow, though it could be: it depends on the plant. I have recently planted a row of *Cortaderia selloana* 'Sunningdale Silver'. A friend dismisses this plant as suburban. But is it suburban when there are five in a row? No, it's fantastic. Solidly, repeatedly, every time I see it, satisfying. What will be added when it flowers? Have to wait and see . . .

I have a small triangular bed with a mix of *Iris sibirica* and crocosmia. Their leaves are very similar and so they blend seamlessly, offering a mass of spiky leaves, set between low box hedges. The irises are gorgeous in early summer – and they really are: they look amazing massed like that, contained by rows of box. Then the crocosmia flowers – only slightly less gorgeous – in late summer. Still a satisfying picture. A friend of mine, Susan Wright, has planted *Crocosmia* 'Lucifer' among a mass of *Leymus arenarius* in a rectangular yard with the path to their front door through the middle. It looks sensational when it flowers. The only other plants are two rows of trimmed beech. They give height and an added dimension. Amazing and classy.

The hint there, too, is the grassy leaves, which not only live seamlessly together but also look good without flower, making crocosmias a good plant to give a seasonal lift to a grass planting. Grasses look wonderful in a large mass, especially

ABOVE LEFT *Iris sibirica* 'Blue King' filling the triangle in June.
ABOVE RIGHT Crocosmia (possibly 'Emily McKenzie') taking over the triangle in August.

if they are open to the wind. No anxiety that they'll get damaged by wind, though a cloudburst can squash some. Add crocosmia or iris, or something else with grassy leaves that I haven't yet thought of, and you have a banker's bonus.

The hosta walk has been moaned about by plant freaks, who want to see fifty different hostas where I have only three, looking almost identical. It's not quite long enough, I think – a bit squat, but pleasing, peaceful. Maybe adding something different along the back will help it balance better? Perhaps. Meanwhile, I'm never quite sure about the flowers and this year removed the ones from *H. sieboldiana* var. *elegans* while tolerating the ones on *H.* 'Halcyon'. Neither is very inspiring and both have to be cut down eventually unless I tolerate them ruining the look of the hostas as they go over. The hostas decay romantically but their flowers do not. Again, it makes a simple planting which works every time for me. I recently visited a much-praised garden which started out not bad. But then every bed and border which followed, being a random mix of herbaceous plants, began to look the same as the last. Any border with only one or two plants would have made a refreshing change.

Simple planting like this has its risks: if one plant fails for some reason you've had it. Nothing's perfect.

SUCCULENTS

'You like your succulents' someone observed one day. How wonderfully patronizing – like 'Old Fred, he do like his pint.' I felt astonished. I'd never thought of the succulents especially possessively, and I hadn't thought whether I was fond of them. But I think I do have to own to this. They are brilliantly sculptural, elegant and sophisticated plants in subtle colours. You need to be able to overwinter them indoors in the UK (people will sometimes manage to keep some of them outside for a few years, but then along will come a real winter and zap them).

They absolutely benefit aesthetically by being repeated. Some make almost identical shapes and so gain by the emphasis that repetition makes; some make weird variations of their own on the general theme and so add that interest which I so admire elsewhere, of small difference within an overall coherence. But, unlike many plants we grow in the UK, they really need empty space around them to display them properly. This makes them good in pots, but a gravel garden could display them well. Just don't try and imitate a desert unless you happen to be living in one.

One of the most dramatic and a deserved favourite is *Aeonium* 'Zwartkop', the one with the dark purple leaves and a tendency to grow long coarse stems, which can make wonderful shapes and shadows in their own right. (Don't ever forget the joy shadows can bring if we ever get some sun.) Bob Brown showed me a neat trick with these aeoniums, which is to take out the very central rosette with a sharp knife: this helps to make it bush out if you prefer that to ever-elongating, elegant stems.

One of my favourites, as a very good-tempered plant among good-tempered plants, is, I believe, *Echeveria runyonii* 'Topsy Turvy'. My lack of certainty about its name is due to the way I have generally sourced these plants – they often turn up in florist's and then often with no labels. That doesn't stop me snapping them up. And propagating them if I can't buy enough at the florist's: in spring the plants often need tiding up because they have developed offsets around the base, spoiling their pristine form – and there you are, lots of baby plants. If there are no offsets, pulling off a leaf and sitting it in a small pot of compost creates an instant effect. The usual advice is to let them dry off for a couple of days before introducing the

An anonymous echeveria.

compost but I don't and seem to be successful anyway.

Plants which need very little water are not as easy as ones which need a lot and which can be left sitting in it. Anxious types like me are always liable to overwater succulents. I once had some beginning to look really miserable so, reluctant to throw them away, I put them in the greenhouse and promptly forgot about them. They stayed there all summer, and although it was a typical global-warming summer – that is, it rained most of the time – they never got a drop of the aforesaid rain or any other water. They looked fine at the end of that.

SCENT

This is a snare and a delusion in the garden. Partly because it is talked up so. People try to persuade you that you could choose the right plants and find yourself surrounded by glorious scent whenever you venture outdoors. No. Most scents require a good sniff, close to. Very few scent the air around them.

Just now (January) you'll find sarcococcas (of several varieties) in flower. Dull little flower. It's one of those that some photographers like to take close-ups of to make you suddenly think there's an amazing flower you'd never registered before – until you get the scale right and realize it's minute. But it pumps out perfume like nobody's business. I can never have too much of a good smell. It lifts my mood instantly, before I've even registered where the good thing that has suddenly happened has come from. And, of course, the nose curiously takes care of any possible overload by shortly refusing to register it any more. I know that violets actually numb the nose after the first sniff, but it seems to me that all smells get handled something like that by the nose. You can enter a room to find quite a horrible pong and then cease to notice it quite soon. Which is why I don't pay heed to the rule that you shouldn't dine with strongly scented flowers in the room, for fear it will kill the flavours of the food. We should be so sensitive.

And that's clearly the problem: I'm not sensitive enough. I can take sockloads of smells if they're good, and never complain. I'm also unusual in loving being surrounded by strong, glorious colour. I cannot understand the preoccupation with white, magnolia and neutrals. They can look great, if carefully selected to work as a coherent whole with a class room, but mostly they just echo dullness. The idea, for lots of people, seems to be that strong colour is too stimulating. Unfortunately I find that, as with scent, it's hard to stay stimulated. Something else takes my attention and I totally fail to go on being gobsmacked. Most absurdly I hear that certain colours should be avoided in the bedroom for fear they will keep you awake and overstimulated. Me, I put the light out.

Meanwhile, sarcococca does the stuff and fills a room or a small garden with scent. Azara can also pack a pretty powerful January smell, and I've just seen what looks like a lying picture of it on the web: a shrub turned yellow with blossom. Well, I've never seen ours like that; you don't notice the flowers, or the shrub, in our garden mostly. But the scent can tell you it's there and that it and you are alive.

I don't pick it – the flowers are so tiny it'd just be sticks in a jar, and you'd have to strip off some of the flower, which goes all down the stem to put it into said jar, and that seems a shame.

What else, actually, cross my heart and hope to die, does scent a room? Not much, for me, except sweet peas when I first bring them in. And they go brown even faster than a snowdrop. Lilies, currently readily and wonderfully available in bud from supermarkets, are overpowering, people say, yet I find I get an occasional wonderful whiff as I pass and create a draught. Lovely, but overwhelmed I am not, just tantalized and teased.

The fact is, I think, that we experience smell differently, just as some of us hear or see better than others, so I take it on trust that some people are overwhelmed by lilies in the house. Presumably those who write books on scent in the garden are more than usually stuck for a topic or have very sensitive noses. Compare noses before you make a 'scented garden'. And remember that scent in a garden sounds like a great topic for a book but that there are only so many scented plants before you start having to stretch things a bit. A friend of mine who is an expert on mushrooms once pointed out that most mushrooms taste of mushroom. Well,

there also are a lot of smells that are hard to differentiate. If you commit to writing a book on scent in the garden you are committing to finding a lot of scented plants to fill up the text.

But in spite of all this scent-lessness in the world, a scented garden has always been quite a popular idea in print and sounds wonderful. There's always a seat, and shelter to 'trap the scent'. There's always a certain lack of reminder that any scent in the garden, apart from those which emerge when you crush a leaf, is very temporary: the year rushes on and that scent is then history until the year has gone round again. And, of course, the real stars of the scented garden tend to have tiny, insignificant white or yellow flowers (see above) so it's not likely to be a visually stunning garden. Better spread them around, I'd say, and then sometimes, unexpectedly, they may astonish and delight you with that lift of spirits that good scent offers.

It's hardly possible to write about scent in the garden without mentioning roses. Currently quite unfashionable in the fashionable garden world, which ought to mean the end of those revolting 'rose gardens' full of naked hybrid teas. It doesn't seem to, however, since fashion in gardens comes in sporadic, random outbreaks, passing most of the world by, like mumps. Even nicer roses, like some of the David Austin English roses, some species and 'old-fashioned' shrub roses, like rugosas, and the wonderful hybrid musks – well, one wonderful hybrid musk to my own knowledge, 'Felicia' – are blobs on bushes with a lovely scent if you can

OPPOSITE *Azara microphylla* in flower in March. Do not be deceived – these flowers are *tiny*.
BELOW LEFT *Rosa* 'Felicia' in June. Full and fragrant and a hybrid musk. More grace in the stems than hybrid teas or floribundas, but still best with legs well covered.
BELOW RIGHT *Rosa* 'François Juranville' (probably), growing over cotoneasters.

Rosa 'Paul's Himalayan Musk' (probably). An exuberant rambler exubing in July.

get your nose in. Trying to hide their ugly legs by sticking them at the back of the border is not a good plan then, unless you also have easy access there too. But still, a vase full of 'Felicia' is a treat.

Shrub roses on the whole have been more trouble than worth to me, apart from 'Felicia', and even she looks pretty sick by September, in time for her second flowering. (Forget it, dear, your age is showing; better take a back seat.) They need a lot of looking after, and as ours don't get that I can't speak for how wonderful they are if they get all the pruning, pest relief, soil replenishing and all the rest of things they'd like. I have gravitated to ramblers – not an indulgence many of us can afford, given how big many of them are. But they are less trouble than their cousins. (Unless, like one of ours, they regularly fall out of the tree on your head.) They are a wonderful sight. Many are supposed to be scented. Guess the birds might notice, but, truly, I never have. Unless there's a flower low enough down to stick my nose in.

HYDRANGEAS

Hydrangeas get sneered at. What to say about such short-sighted prejudice? Just notions, as usual, I imagine, empty ideas arising out of an image problem. You can just about get away with appreciating lacecaps, the sophisticated hydrangea, but mopheads are a bit like the scullery maids their name conjures up, totally *déclassé*.

Ignore all that. They are all great plants, if for no other reason than they flower for months, fading imperceptibly through a range of subtle, gorgeous colours. You can get little ones – for pots maybe? – and great big ones and everything in between. Buy the little ones on sight and in flower if you can afford them, and then take cuttings (easy) and make a dramatic display that will see you possibly from July into October. Fit the bigger ones in if you can, lavishly, of course. And go to see the little courtyard at Burford House, Worcestershire, to see *Hydrangea aspera* Villosa Group lifting a small garden into the ranks of the very best.

You can make an informal garden-dividing hedge of them, or make telling accents of colour that delightfully complement the beginnings of autumn. You can have a couple of pots of them matching each other on either side of your front door. You could make a whole large bed of them in similar colours, playing with the subtlety of those colours, which could enrich each other with slight differences while also offering a solid unity.

There are things people love to go on about, about hydrangeas. The variability of flower colour depending on the acidity of the soil. The fact that the flowers aren't flowers but modified leaves called 'bracts'. This last is useful to remember, maybe, because it's why the flowers are so long-lasting, like hellebores. You can look all that up. Go and play.

SHARING A GARDEN

Sharing a garden is not good, even if it's with your most beloved. And it shows. Couples who both contribute cheerfully and randomly to their garden's design leave their trails behind them rather like slugs. You can see where the 'cutting-edge steel and concrete' person has been and where the 'cottage garden and chaos' person has been. You can see where the decorator has been allowed to creep over the 'keep it pure and simple'. It sometimes isn't as crude or obvious as these examples suggest: sometimes it just emerges in greater confusion than there would otherwise have been.

I began the garden with Charles's help. That rapidly came to remind me of the way that when I was a child I never really felt 'my' room was mine at all, since people would tell me to tidy it up and generally throw their weight around in it. (I never got over being told to tidy my room on my *birthday*: unforgivable.) And because it wasn't mine I never really identified with it or personalized it as I have subsequently with homes that really have been mine. So how could I expect Charles to identify with the garden and feel part of it, when what he was doing was 'helping'?

So it seemed obvious that he would need a 'place of his own': I 'donated' the veg plot in a small ceremony involving a copy of *The Vegetable Expert*, a key and a photograph. In the photograph Charles looks bemused.

But he took it on, and the rule is this: you may consult the other, and indeed anyone else, but in your 'territory' you make the final decision. Simple and effective. It hasn't stopped us having rows on occasions, because garden design is a very sensitive area. When someone wades in, even by invitation, and begins to make suggestions you inevitably want to hit them. Things become precious which were never precious before, and with that you become precious as well. It is as if someone is about to rob you: and indeed they are. We're usually talking destruction of some kind, even of just a notion, and that in itself is painful. But it helps if you feel confident that you are the final arbiter of what will or won't happen.

Dividing the garden does not solve everything. Housekeeping has been an issue. Many garden visitors are preoccupied with outdoor housekeeping. And I regret to acknowledge, because I have no wish to say negative things about a man I love totally, that Charles was once responsible too for exacerbating the misery of

A view over the yew gardens to the grasses parterre on the far slope, with yew pillars in the foreground in need of clipping.

this demand. Until we adopted the 'if you mention it, it's your job' rule. We still have to issue each other with reminders, though. Sigh.

That kind of difficulty arises out of differences of temperament and inclination. Charles has always been more concerned with tidiness in the garden than I am and we settled this in the end – perhaps the end – by acknowledging that keeping paths clear and tidy sets everything else off well. Similarly, keeping hedges trim provides the essential edge that makes a slight chaos elsewhere a satisfying contrast.

Charles has also always had an ability to deal with detail. This makes him ideal support when it comes to the tax return and it made his 'potager' period in the veg plot a delight. It also tends to make him impatient with my 'broad sweeps' approach. But step away from the potential for conflict and then you can see the benefit: one partner into broad sweeps and the other into detail means that both those aspects of the garden, and of life together, can be addressed properly and creatively.

I made the garden thinking of the broad strokes and the scope for fun and expression. To make satisfying shapes in three dimensions and create sights to be seen. The yew and beech hedges sitting in the valley making shapes that I dreamt of and now can see. To make a pool that would reflect – what? To say something about the place and about the surrounding countryside. And, yes, to grow plants and mass them in wonderful sweeps and repeats. And even have those ephemeral, tantalizing and frustrating glories – flowers. Had I been preoccupied with detail I would never have had those dreams or been able to tolerate the chaos on the way to realizing them. (Charles had to look the other way a great deal.)

I did not, however, think about condemning myself to outside housework for the rest of my life. I had thought that the jokes about old maiden aunts who run their fingers along the shelf to find the dust were as obsolete as maiden aunts, but, believe me, it seems they haunt us still in the form of people obsessed with weeds and 'tidiness'. The management of a garden affects its appearance and atmosphere. This is actually far from a simple issue. Important but rarely discussed. If you share a garden you have to find a management style you both can live with, and this means discussing it as a management style and not as a character flaw on the part of your partner.

I have seen gardens gardened within an inch of their lives. I have seen gardens so 'tidy' it makes your soul cringe. The kind of garden where the lawns are 'edged' with a special tool, designed to keep the grass and the plants forever apart and weeded to death. Such gardens prickle with discomfort and control.

Not that tidiness is necessarily and inevitably anathema. A minimalist town garden, with clean lines and restrained planting, needs careful maintenance, just as such a room in the house would be demanding.

The suburban garden has its own special place; perhaps an element of the blowsy and bucolic characterizes many, and such a feel needs a little looseness round the edges, a feeling that nature is not totally dominated and tidied away. A country garden even more so, especially round the edges. This garden especially benefits the landscape it is in if it defers to it a little and shares some of the nature of the countryside it is in. But again, it must depend on the effect the garden-maker is aiming for and this is even harder to generalize about. But who, doing their sniffy number about weeds or whatever, ever stops to ask themselves just what is being attempted here? Does this – whatever it is that is so very upsetting – add or detract from that effect? Do I actually understand this garden?

We have struggled with this issue and we have come to some conclusions about what we want. Certain areas need to be weed-free here – the paths, for example. The paths need to be clear so that people can walk through the garden unmolested and freely: which is why after every rainstorm I am out in the garden cutting down all the branches of trees and shrubs which have been beaten down and now obstruct the headway. (However hard back they are cut the need to do this job still recurs two or three times a year.)

The paths need to be kept clear too, almost everywhere, for the contrast they offer in their plainness to the colour and comparative chaos of the flowering plants, and for the way they complement the hedges. Wherever possible we like to see the soil mulched, knowing this is good for the plants, good for the soil and helpful in limiting weed-seeding. Aesthetically it provides a pleasing background to any plants which have not filled the space. Which is interesting to think about in itself – do we always want plants cheek by jowl? Sometimes I wonder whether the price of never enjoying the sight of the form and shape of the plant is rather a high price to pay. Pots provide that opportunity – though some people turn those into an unholy mess too – but why only pots? The grasses parterre has offered some possibilities here, with some grasses spaced apart from each other and regularly mulched. It is interesting to consider how far apart you might want grasses to grow from each other in order to display their form without their beginning to look lost and unrelated. Mulching makes this effect possible, so that the repetition of the same fountaining grass over a wide area pleases in quite a different way from a similar grass simply massed.

Tulips display fabulously well like this – and being so early can pop up in an empty flower bed with bare soil around them before the masses turn up. Not that I have tried this, for well-rehearsed reasons.

This is a long way from garden sharing. In summary, we are fortunate to have room to divide the garden between us and also to share broadly similar tastes. In a smaller garden I'm not sure how you do it, but you have to work some system out if the garden is going to be content.

And if you have children as well? Give up and leave it fifteen years.

THE WOODS

The woods are part of the garden and not part of the garden. They are where the wild things are – squirrels, rabbits, deer, maybe wild pigs and maybe even panthers – and we wish they weren't. The wild things make their way over the fence sometimes, causing alarm and despondency.

So the woods get separated off by fencing and gates and this leads to them feeling separate and 'outside'. It takes deliberate thought to go to the woods and it isn't part of the usual garden tour for us or our visitors. Two acres of fairly intense garden is more than enough for one visit.

We go to the woods at special times and we go there to walk through to the forest beyond. I was once full of distress and needed to walk. The man who used to sort out the verges was working the lane, making drainage channels to keep it dry, cutting things back and doing similar useful work. The council used to deliver him together with his little shelter, which they moved further down the lane each day as his work progressed, and he told me he wrote up what he had seen in his diary every day. I wonder what became of that? He retired and naturally was not replaced.

The woods, principally beech in this part.

Anyway, I knew he was in the lane and it was impossible to pass him without speaking, which was an intolerable thought given the state I was in. But through the woods I could walk without risk of encountering anyone. How is that for privilege? And it has always been the woods that non- gardening men have envied: it clearly hits some part of the psyche in some profound way, the idea of owning a wood. Though of all parts of our land we feel we own this least: it is too undomesticated to feel 'owned' in fact. That is probably its power.

Charles was clearly one of those men who felt that owning a wood was possibly as special as owning a sports car, and possibly more classy. Or else he just wanted access to the firewood. It was he who pestered the Forestry Commission persistently until they gave in and let us buy it. It was such a discreet piece of woodland – almost precisely a square about two acres in size, attached at one side to our land and to the forestry at the other. We had an anxious day when the Forestry Commission demanded reassurance that the neighbours who owned the fields on the other two sides didn't want to buy it, but they didn't and it became ours. Or, rather, Charles's.

It had had 'experimental Japanese larch' growing in it, planted in the 1870s. We met someone whose father had had the job of going to measure the circumference of the trees in the 1950s, so presumably the experiment continued being of interest to someone. But these trees had at last been cut before we arrived, leaving enormous stumps behind (great for planting ferns into – they seem to like the moist rot) and many standard trees which had survived alongside them to grow enormously straight and tall: oak, beech and hornbeam. Following this cut a variety of trees were rapidly regenerating – birch, elm, yew, hazel, holly, sorbus, viburnum and more hornbeam: a wonderful variety.

Until the time we managed to buy it we had been scavenging it anyway. When we first arrived and everything needed doing everywhere, I found myself dragooned into wheeling barrowloads of wood into the shed while Charles cut up the forestry leavings from the Japanese larch. We invested in a couple of wood-burners which have provided our central heating ever since. (And, no, that does not mean they heat a boiler: it just means they're in the middle of the house.)

By the time we had bought it the wood in summer had been taken over by bracken and bramble. I set off one day to try to make a path through to the far side, working my way through with a pair of shears. It all closed up behind me and suddenly in the middle I was afraid: I was totally surrounded by unpleasant foliage which was above my head. I couldn't see where I had come from or where I was going. Of such experiences fairy stories were born. Curiously I sometimes recapture that feeling in late summer in the middle of the crescent border, which does the same trick of growing taller than me and letting me in, and then offering no obvious way out.

So for years I killed bracken and bramble and, apart from right now, when it's coming back and I should really be out there dealing with it, we have made the woods accessible. Perhaps too much so, because in that process we lost the entire understorey – there are trees and a lot of empty ground underneath. It doesn't yet look quite as I intend.

Which is? Well, I hate British woodland filled with foreign fare. I cannot justify this, at least not on ecological grounds: I happen to have been told by a researcher who should know that our British native wildlife does fine on foreign food (you'd know it from the way the birds stuff themselves on peanuts). It's not objectionable on aesthetic grounds either, necessarily – trees with herbaceous plants underneath can look great. Even fat-leaved hostas and brightly coloured primulas. Why not? (Well, maybe not.)

My attachment to a wood full of lots of standard trees with bluebells and shrubs underneath is not really defensible. Historically woods didn't look at all like that. Woods were often coppiced and a wood where all the trees have been coppiced

really confronts our expectations of how a wood should look – all those shrub-like trees. When hardwood trees are cut for coppice you can count on an outcry from local people, who frequently believe that the way to kill a tree is to cut it down. Next time you come across a developer who believes he has got rid of that wonderful oak despite the tree preservation order he blithely ignored, see if you can get him compelled to leave it to regenerate. You won't have too long to wait to have your tree back, if in rather a different form. A form that would offer good firewood in a few years, after which it could start the regrowth all over again, over and over for centuries.

Pollarded trees might seem

The woods in snow, in January.

more familiar – it at least has a trunk (called in this use a bolling) up to some height above six feet, where it sprouts a coppice stool, cut that high to prevent grazing animals (and where are they in our stereotype wood?) eating the regrowth. Then what about shredded trees? That is a system of 'cropping the side branches of a tree leaving a tuft on top' (Oliver Rackham, *History of the Countryside* – read it: wonderful). How weird is that? Is that what you expect to see in a wood: a bare-stemmed tree with a tuft on top?

So what do I intend our wood to look like and why? What I want is actually a pastiche wood. A wood that looks how we think a wood ought to look. A lot of standard trees of varying ages. Undergrowth, but not too much of it for fear we couldn't walk through comfortably. Bluebells, of course. Yes! We got them – clearing the bracken and bramble brought us bluebells, and every year they spread further and further through the wood. So, not too much undergrowth either or the bluebells won't get a look in.

And this pastiche is just about what we have got. And however satisfactory and 'normal' it looks – no one comes out saying 'what a funny wood, why does it look like that?' – it worries us a little because it is so useless. We have some fine beeches, oaks and hornbeams, all far too big to cut down and some of them at the edge of their life. Lovely trees – when we have gales, especially in autumn when the beeches are still in leaf, I dread getting up to a transformed landscape where the beeches have gone over, throwing their broad shallow root plate in the air.

What we need, and many of our predecessors may have needed too, is actually smallish wood near ground level at a size we can reasonably cut and bring in for firewood. Coppice in fact. But cutting our commonest regenerated and not too enormous tree, the hornbeam, is no joke at any size. It is a saw blunter. We would love to look forward to a secure old age with guaranteed, easily accessible firewood ensuring we can afford to keep warm. Instead we have a lot of enormous and useless if very beautiful old trees.

So, given those preoccupations and these existing constraints, what have we done? We will draw a veil over Charles's fun plantings of ornamental trees which mostly died. And his (sorry, Charles) somewhat bizarre planting of young trees in among the stronger, much healthier and more cheerful regenerating forms of the same things. I wouldn't mention it but he's in good company. People like planting trees more it seems than nurturing much more robust regenerating seedlings and saplings.

What I decided I could live with was some grouping of trees, which we often achieved by removal of what didn't fit with the group. We already had a vast swathe of beech. We now began to encourage a sorbus group, a birch group and a holly walk. It just about works. I thought I did not want colours which would look

Erythronium 'Pagoda' fills the woods in April, so far surviving all wildlife (fingers crossed).

strange and alien, but that white and pale yellow could maybe look good in this context. So for a buzz I planted four or five *Viburnum plicatum* 'Lanarth' or 'Mariesii' (forget which) in a rough group under the sorbus. I have this vision of coming across a froth of pure white layers of flower unexpectedly among the trees. Hasn't happened yet but it's on the way, if the squirrels, deer and rabbit spare the plan.

I also added some *Ribes sanguineum* 'Tydeman's White' in a group for a similar if not quite so romantic effect. Watering them in the following drought was no joke as the nearest tap is a very long way downhill. Hope they will come to something too.

Then just one other thing: every autumn Charles plants fifty or so *Erythronium* 'Pagoda'. They seem to be the one bulb apart from bluebells that doesn't get eaten or otherwise destroyed. And every spring, before the bluebells and before we have any visitors but friends, we have the private delight of seeing an increasing woodland spread of delicate, if surprisingly large, bell-like pale yellow flowers. This variety sadly doesn't seed, but the clumps get bigger. One mad friend, garden writer Stephen Anderton, betrays his total lack of understanding of the economy of the garden and the work that it demands: he insists we should dig them up and split them. They cost (now – and were cheaper) £35 a hundred. We're not rich, so £17.50 is not nothing . . . but, well, words fail me. Seems to me the easiest option is to keep affording them while we can and as a plan it's going very well. If you want to dig and split rather than sit and read a good book please feel free.

VISITORS

Visitors come in several different varieties. Some see the garden for free, some even get bed and board, some have to pay and come at special times, and some get refused entry having turned up at the wrong time. This is not a new problem for those anxious to visit houses or gardens. In *Consuming Passions: Leisure and Pleasure in Victorian Britain* Judith Flanders quotes a would-be visitor to Wroxton Abbey complaining that 'I prevailed upon my party to drive down to it; when unluckily for us Lord G. was just arrived from London, and denied us admittance. Very rude this . . . Let him either forbid his place entirely; open it always [sic]; or else fix a day of admission: but, for shame, don't refuse travellers who may have come 20 miles out of their way for a sight of the place . . .'

But we do have opening times and wistful people begging to be admitted at other times, and this is not new either.

> Mr Walpole is very ready to oblige any curious persons with the sight of his house and collection; but as it is situated so near to London and in so populous a neighbourhood, and as he refuses a ticket to nobody that sends for one, it is but reasonable that such persons as send, should comply with the rules he has been obliged to lay down for showing it.
>
> Any person, sending a day or two before, may have a ticket for four persons for a certain day . . . If more than four persons come with a ticket, the housekeeper has positive orders to admit none of them . . .
>
> As Mr Walpole has given offence by sometimes enlarging the number of four, and refusing that latitude to others, he flatters himself that for the future nobody will take it ill that he strictly confines the number; as whoever desires him to break his rule, does in effect expect him to disoblige others, which is what nobody has a right to desire him . . . If any person does not make use of the ticket, Mr Walpole hopes he shall have notice; otherwise he is prevented from obliging others on that day, and thence is put to great inconvenience.

Similarly the exasperating way visitors respond to a garden when they are invited in is wonderfully echoed by Dickens's description of Mr Guppy and friend visiting a stately home:

Mr Guppy and his friend are dead beat before they have well begun. They straggle about in wrong places, look at wrong things, don't care for the right things . . . exhibit profound depression of spirits . . .

So, given all that inconvenience, administration and lack of appreciation, why do we open at all?

Well, how could I not open the garden? The garden is ours, made for the two of us for sure, but it is also a communication with the world, a pleasure that I want to offer to other people's hearts, eyes and minds. Unshared it would become pointless and self-indulgent. And impossibly expensive.

We need the money we take from charging for admission to help pay for the garden: it is an incredibly expensive thing to run, even though we do most of the work ourselves. Just the hedge-cutting – even with a healthy (in every sense) contribution from us – costs a fortune, never mind the cost of running, servicing and replacing machines like lawnmowers, wheelbarrows, strimmers and hedge-cutters. Weedkillers, slug killers, potting compost, paint, pool dye – all cost money.

Or at least they do as long as we can get them. The EU did its best to destroy our seed bank by dictating that all seeds which are sold must be 'distinct, uniform and stable varieties'. For seed merchants to certify them as such is prohibitively expensive, so many old and rare varieties, not to mention meadow wildflowers, are directly threatened and only currently protected by charitable organizations. Now the EU is after our herbicides and insecticides. The kind of knee-jerk 'all -icides are *bad*' (they sound bad, don't they?) not only makes the media uninterested in this scandal but no doubt informed the EU vote. Food prices will rise, as will cheaper imports of food from countries with more sense or poor regulation. And my gardening will get more labour-intensive, if not impossible.

Meanwhile, if you open, everyone has their hand in your till; you're regarded as fair game. Opening for the National Gardens Scheme is essential – the vast majority of garden visits are made from the *Yellow Book*, and the only way to be in the *Yellow Book* is to open for the NGS.

This can be a problem for us, because people leap at the idea of coming for charity rather than helping out impecunious owners, so when we opened on a Sunday (the only right day for the particular religion of garden visiting) for the NGS we would get swamped by visitors and be totally unable to park them, having space for only ten cars in our car park. On days when we have opened for the garden funds we have had people drive in, enquire whether we are open for charity and discovering that we aren't turn round and drive off. Presumably they do the same when they visit the cinema. Or do they manage to live without supporting any business?

Many people have friendly supportive neighbours who make teas, man the gates and offer their fields for parking. You hear all about them whenever the NGS is mentioned. Well, you don't have neighbours like that in the Veddw. Several of our neighbours hate our openings and some who will be nameless but should know better even go in for sabotage, sending one couple – who had come from Canada – off on a totally wild goose chase when they asked where we were.

The neighbours who did kindly grant us use of their field, for a charitable contribution, watched the visitors through their binoculars and complained about their parking habits – and, worse, they have had the misfortune to have to haul people out of the field with their tractor in reward for their generosity when it has rained. People seem to believe we are in control of our visitors, which sounds quite right and quite as it should be until you wonder how we are supposed to make people do things outside our garden boundaries when we are confined within, attending to other visitors. If people sort of do as they think fit, and then set off round the garden, how are we to locate or identify the culprits?

We are almost at the end of our lane, or the beginning, depending on which way you're going, so people don't really drive past our neighbours in vast disruptive numbers, but we are resented for it, it seems, by all those who were here before us. Later comers to the lane don't seem to mind so much and they are slowly becoming the majority of the inhabitants.

So we are caught between the NGS, who wish us to fill their coffers at the expense of our coffers, on the one hand; and the impossibility of staying loved enough by our neighbours to earn the privilege of inconveniencing them with the necessity to mow their field, tolerate cars and nosey people in said field and offer dramatic tractor rescues. We were unpopular on both sides whatever we did. We resolved this by having evening openings, which offer people the absolute best time to see the garden if it's not raining but which never produce the unparkable hordes. We can be lucky to get thirty visitors. This way we are just hated, and reprimanded, by the NGS County Organizer.

And could we pay a fixed sum of money to the NGS for an entry in the *Yellow Book* instead? No.

The RHS brought us different headaches when they designated us an 'RHS recommended garden'. In order to have the publicity and status they offer we had to have their members in for free. This led on occasions to such irritations as having a couple turning up in separate cars, using up two of our scarce parking spaces and getting two of our free guides all for nothing in the till. That wouldn't be so bad if they weren't so smug and tactlessly gleeful about getting in free. I wonder if perhaps they thought that the RHS pay us something for letting their members in for nothing? The RHS system works well, as indeed the NGS system does too, for those garden owners who add extras and make some money for themselves or their garden that way: teas, lunches, plant sales, sundries and twee garden-associated products.

We are not really a business, though of course as far as the Inland Revenue is concerned we are. I discovered this for sure when a friend who knew about marketing referred to our 'product'. We're an exception and a rarity – people who open regularly in order to survive financially but who don't have the time or resources to turn opening the garden into a full-time concern. The Veddw is a private garden which we share with the world.

It is critical that it is our garden, which is the expression of our thoughts, our feelings, our relationship to the place – and it is the result of that dynamic that we are sharing with the public, rather vulnerably, not a business. It feels to me in some important ways that if we were to turn it into a business, and to turn me into a tea lady, that would somehow betray the whole essence of the place, besides depriving us of the joy of it in peace and quiet much of the time. Here I risk being slapped down for being precious. No matter. I believe that it is a good offer to make to the world, the best I can.

To be slightly more concrete: someone said to me once, perfectly straight, 'If you're going to open it to the public, are you going to start putting in bedding plants?' In a way they were quite right. If we really wanted to make money we wouldn't make *our* garden: we would design and make a garden which we imagined would please popular taste and fit in nicely with the scones and teacakes. It's madness commercially to make an idiosyncratic garden, without plant labels; indeed without a focus on a vast variety of different plants and none of them for sale. Never mind no teas and not for charity either.

We make no sense to most people, then – neither commercial nor charitable. We maintain our tradition as outsiders even in this regard.

NEW MEDIA

It was a form of deference, long after deference had supposedly died out. If some editor included an article in a newspaper or serious magazine, I tended to trust their judgement, assume there was a good reason for it to be there and passively read it. The corrosion of this attitude began a long time ago now, for me, when I became bored stiff by the garden stuff in papers and magazines and finally by the garden magazines in their entirety. Now I find that response spreading because at the back of my mind a corrosive question is lurking: would I click this link?

This is directly the result of Twitter. Twitter is like a party full of interesting people. You can wander around, eavesdropping, occasionally joining in a conversation, sometimes entering an energetic debate. There are people there whose world is totally foreign to me and (special this) it is often unclear how old they are or of what social class or race. Broadly speaking the people I choose to follow must have something in common with me. The sad fact is that although I follow practically every gardener on the site they are often the dullest of the lot. The US gardeners glow with enthusiasm, sentimentality and garden advice. The British gardeners tend to display their national characteristics of facetiousness, irrelevance and banter. But this is not static and I think as more gardeners join in the debate, serious discussion and mutual help will grow. Bloggers are a mixed bunch but there are serious writers out there and there is serious co-operation and exchange developing.

But the point for me is that on Twitter I choose what to read and who to talk to. People's tweets are often like little flags they're waving: 'Read my blog' is the commonest theme, best with some taster to tempt. I don't click the links to many, as the tasters tell me clearly all I need to know about the originality on offer – it's often about plants or hackneyed advice of the kind that every garden magazine and newspaper is full of. But – unlike with a newspaper or book – you can instantly say 'hey, you can't do that!' and a dialogue begins.

So I have small patience left with deference to editors. I've become my own editor.

I click the links to the best garden blogs, and to politics, science, history, archaeology, culture (which is the aspect of gardens which is missing most) and girly trivia for the fun. And to things recommended by people I know who are interesting and who will take me interesting places.

Garden blogs are very interesting because they are certainly the challenge that dreary garden magazines will have to begin to take note of. Some bloggers are beginning to visit gardens and then write what they thought of them, complete with illustrative (not necessarily flattering) pictures. There is still a lot of garden flattery but a harder, clearer-eyed view is beginning to emerge. Bloggers no doubt feel that they owe their readers the courtesy of honesty, though there's still too much reliance on 'I liked' and 'I didn't like' without explanation. People comment, freely, on the blog content; a little way from the magazine letters page with its statutory 'I love this magazine' star letter, their comments are just occasionally confrontational.

I also edit the thinkingardens website, even it if now seems such an old-fashioned form (if nothing like as old-fashioned as a book!). It seems a good way to bring really good and interesting garden writing to the garden interested.

In 2006 a small group of us, with support at arm's length from the Royal Horticultural Society, formed a ginger group for gardens, which we call thinkingardens. A ginger group is defined in a web dictionary as 'a group within, for example, a political party, seeking to inspire the rest with its own enthusiasm and activity', which is exactly what we're about. We've had ambitious plans but never enough money to really achieve them or people with the time to make things happen, so we rather stagger along. We've started having regular suppers in the winter where about a dozen garden-interested people meet to discuss serious garden topics over good food and drink: I love it and it is always lively, loud and entertaining. And we did get from the RHS funding for the website, which I have been running since we began.

I hardly knew what to do with it at first, but recognized that we needed something to read besides our 'mission statement'. So I began begging and borrowing material from anyone I half-knew in the garden world and the response, if slow to get away, has become amazing. The site is becoming a huge archive of interesting articles on all the aspects of gardens that never get discussed in the usual garden media, all given free by some of the best garden writers of our time. Exciting.

Before the Internet we would probably have wanted to create a magazine in order to put our ideas out. And we wouldn't have been able to afford it, either in time or money. A website's not quite as yummy as a magazine – I doubt people read their netbooks in the bath – but technology is constantly changing and bath-proof tech may soon be with us.

Unlike a magazine, a website acts as an archive, so instead of an expensive, throwaway paper magazine you can have an accumulating set of papers. Most of the kind of articles we've got on the site don't date and there are no recycling worries. As the site grew, so did the readership and so thinkingardens exists and thrives through the website, come rain or shine. Well, as long as I reign and shine.

I find the new media and new tech exciting and challenging. It can take time to work out the best uses to make of these new opportunities and, of course, there are worries about the cost, as in where will people make the money on the web to pay writers and photographers? Far too many people are writing for free; but that has sometimes led to them getting good offers of work in the printed media. It is notable that the person making best use of the web for a newspaper was herself recruited on the basis of her blog. Too many editors of print media seem unable to quite understand the opportunities. But what is most striking as I sit here writing this is that I know it will take over eighteen months for this to reach the public – and what will have happened to technology and the web in that time? This piece will have all the interest of an historic document.

EXILE AND BELONGING

The garden in many ways sums up for me one of the major discomforts of my life: the longing for home and the permanent exclusion from home. Home in this sense involves more than simply a place. Within that notion lie family, friendship, belonging and history, all tied together. And anyone who knows me will spot the contradiction: I have pushed individualism farther than most and am not very 'family'. Indeed, chose not to have one.

I abandoned my home town early in my adult life – so far so ordinary – and with it, for many years, my original family. Once you have left you can return, but it will be, for both good and ill, on very different terms. It will never again be that seamless, mindless, taken-for-granted belonging. And neither, of course, will you be taken for granted in a seamless, mindless way.

I have since attempted to create new places to belong to and new families from friends and colleagues, but ultimately anyone who embraces freedom also is forced to acknowledge that that freedom is the death of belonging: there is no security in free relationships. Friends can suddenly decide to emigrate and we all know that lovers can betray.

Nor, for me, is there a real sense of belonging in a place where neither I nor my ancestors were born.

Nationalism slaps those of us who have moved to a different country in the face with our inability to belong. I live in Wales now, and will always be English and outsider, conscious of a rejection of and contempt for the English which is for many part of the very lifeblood of being Welsh. But that is only a larger expression of the fact that I have left my birthplace and needed to leave my birthplace. England is not that birthplace, because by its very nature a birthplace is small and local. Nationalism is a kind of substitute for many people but they will frequently find that another part of their 'country' is as foreign to them as a foreign country. The British Isles in particular have an enormously varied landscape, so that those of us whose sense of belonging is intimately tied up with landscape will find foreignness within an hour's drive.

And then, worse, I have not only attempted to make a home where I do not belong, but I have made a garden here – shaped and re-created the land I live on, made it my own while always knowing I am transient, with neither ancestor or

Looking past the crescent border up the yew walk to the coppice in snow.

descendants in this place. I have 'owned' my predecessors here; owned in the sense of acknowledging, and owned in the sense of 'taking ownership of' – by incorporating, embodying and including their presence in the garden I have made on their land. And hopefully by paying homage to their lives and work in this place.

I have also attempted to make my home in the garden world, yet remain an outsider. My attempts to find work, and my fierce rejection of the way the media works; my struggles to be accepted while all the while shouting the unacceptable – these sum up the conflicts and contradictions of the need for unthinking belonging and the need for freedom.

Perhaps the place where the struggle is nearest to being resolved is in my marriage, a relationship played out in a home shared but with separate living quarters, offering intimacy and freedom. Not many dare to enjoy the delights of separate beds, so universally, it seems, seen as the sign of a dead marriage: while the shared bed, of farts, snores and the tyranny of 'lights out', seems like a living nightmare to me. The pleasures of privacy and enhanced autonomy strengthen intimacy and sharing.

In all of this I am ordinary. All these conflicts between belonging and freedom are the playing out of the place we as a society have dropped ourselves in and are the price we are paying for the escape from the confines of duty, tradition and rootedness. We wander the earth as restless tourists, searching for who knows what, full of puritanical injunctions about everything but with nothing in the place of a true moral ground. And all that contradiction and tension is here in my garden, expressed in it, experienced in it and never giving peace.

BIBLIOGRAPHY

Collins, John, *The Celts: Origins, Myths Inventions*, Tempus Publishing Ltd, 2003

Cran, Marion, *The Garden of Ignorance: The Experiences of A Woman in a Garden*, Herbert Jenkins, 1924

Fish, Margery, *We Made a Garden*, new edition Faber and Faber, 1983

Flanders, Judith, *Consuming Passions: Leisure and Pleasure in Victorian Britain*, paperback edition Harper Perennial, 2007

Foley, 'An evolutionary and chronological framework for human social behaviour', *Proceedings of the British Academy* 88: 95–117, 1996

Gabb, James Ashe, *A Brief Memoir of James Davies: Master of the National School, on Devauden-Hill, Monmouthshire*, SPCK, 1849; new edition Bibliobazaar, 2009

Gilpin, William, *Observations on the River Wye*, new edition Pallas Athene Arts, 2005

Golden, James, 'View from Federal Twist', http://federaltwist.blogspot.com/

Hay, Roy, *The Gardening Year*, Reader's Digest, 1976

James, Simon, *The Atlantic Celts*, British Museum Press, 1999

Jekyll, Gertrude, *Colour Schemes for the Flower Garden*, new edition Frances Lincoln, 1987

Lane Fox, Robin, *Better Gardening*, David R. Godine, 1986

Lloyd, Christopher, with Tom Bennett, *Clematis*, revised edition Viking, 1989

O'Brien, Constance, *The Guild of Garden Lovers*, new edition 2010

Rackham, Oliver, *History of the Countryside*, Weidenfeld & Nicolson, 1994

Sackville-West, Vita, *In Your Garden*, new edition Frances Lincoln, 2004

Stout, R., *How to have a Green Thumb without an Aching Back: A New Method of Mulch Gardening*, Exposition Press, 1955

Sylvester, Dorothy, *The rural landscape of the Welsh Borderland: a study in historical geography*, Macmillan, 1969

Thomas, Graham Stuart, *Plants for Ground Cover*, revised edition Weidenfeld & Nicolson, 1990

Toomey, Mary, and Everett Leeds, *An Illustrated Encyclopaedia of Clematis*, Timber Press, 2001

ACKNOWLEDGEMENTS

This book only came about as the result of a garden, which means that so many people who helped make the garden possible are to be thanked.

Neither the garden nor the book would be here at all without the hard work and loving support of my husband, Charles Hawes, and my endless, essential dialogue with him. Small words for the depth of the life task it has turned out to be for us. He also contributed the brilliant pictures. Having failed endlessly to capture the garden with a camera myself, I know very well what skill it takes to do that.

In our early days here Anne Dixon-Child provided endless wonderful plants, and Jessica Hawes weeded remorselessly and gave other vital help. My father, Dennis Wharton, has also given emergency support on several depressing occasions. (Drainage, for example.)

Steve Beale came to help out with his meticulous hedge-cutting, tree-felling and sheer muscle as the garden began to demand more input than we were able to manage alone.

He has been followed lately by Jeff Green – a man to lean on and born to be a gardener. I can no longer contemplate trying to manage the Veddw without his sensitive and reliable hard work.

Sara Maitland's faith in the garden kept me going for long, bleak years. She has offered critical help – in all the best senses – with this book, and is the best, wisest and most generous of friends.

Susan Wright and Bridget Rosewell are real lookers. They give me the best gift a gardener can have – they really do see the garden. There is nothing more rewarding than seeing someone, on their own, just standing and looking. And sometimes they make perceptive and illuminating criticisms, which benefit the garden.

Stephen Anderton is a looker too and has caused important changes in the garden. He also kindly went out of his way to encourage my earliest writing and initiated the creation of thinkingardens, which in itself has also helped keep me going during low times. And Chris Young has shared good times and bad, an understanding, constant friend.

Joanna Fortnam and Jane Perrone have been both encouraging and helpful with the book.

We are grateful to Caitriona Cartwright, stonemason, who made our 'Memorial Stones', and to Elsa and Adrian Woods, who used to run an excellent nursery, where they gave plants away for free (well, at least they did to me). I am grateful for that and other kindnesses from them.

Tweeting gets an often ill-informed and poor press from those who don't enjoy it, but the tweeps are a constant source of delight – and have provided an instant research source for this book. In addition, twitter brought me Karen Wilde, who transformed both the Veddw and the thinkingardens websites for me, and has hand-held me through using them, and Elizabeth Buckley, who generously created the beautiful and meticulous garden plan.

I am grateful too to those generous garden visitors who have offered more than 'lovely garden'.

Finally, of course, I want to thank Andrew Dunn and Jo Christian for their courage in publishing this rather problematic book, and patience in dealing with this rather problematic writer; Becky Clarke for the cheerfully bad-tempered jacket; and Nicki Davis for so elegantly bringing together my words and Charles's pictures.

INDEX